THE 5 ROLES OF LEADERSHIP

Tools & best practices for personable
and effective leaders

WLADISLAW JACHTCHENKO

Remote Publishing
www.remote-verlag.de

For questions and comments:
info@remote-verlag.de

First edition 2021 Remote Life LLC, Oakland Park, FL.

Cover design and book layout: Wolkenart–Marie-Katharina Wölk
Translation and proofreading: Gateway Translations Inc.
Editorial Team: Maximilian Mika
Graphics: Marie Mika

ISBN Print: 978-1-955655-17-0

For more information about the publisher, please visit: **www.remote-verlag.de**

Table of contents

Leadership as a Multidimensional Task

Being a leader is a multidimensional task. Effective leaders embody and master the five roles that great leadership entails in any industry:

ROLE 1: **The Convincing Communicator**

ROLE 2: **The Effective Manager**

ROLE 3: **The Motivating Team Leader**

ROLE 4: **The Empathetic Psychologist**

ROLE 5: **The Skilled Problem Solver**

This book will empower you to integrate these five roles into your daily work life and become the most effective and personable leader you can be.

As the **Convincing Communicator**, you're charismatic in convincing your employees and business partners in any situation. To do that you need the body language and voice of a leader as well as argumentative persuasion techniques you can apply to convince others of your point of view. Communication is never a one-way street, however, so superb listening skills are also part and parcel of every successful leader's rhetorical repertoire. As a professional communicator, you create an open feedback culture in your organization. You communicate values and visions in a way that leaves your employees motivated and eager to come to work. This section provides you with the rhetorical tools you need to master everyday communication with confidence (*on page 11*).

As the **Effective Manager**, you are always effective and efficient in your work. And with the help of the proven techniques presented in this book, you'll be able to increase your output without ever overworking yourself. These techniques for effectiveness and efficiency are easily integrated into your everyday life, and several practical exercises help you solidify them as the new norm for productivity (*on page 43*).

As the **Team Leader**, you effortlessly motivate your team and delegate appropriate tasks to your employees. You set clear directions and ensure that company plans are successfully implemented, even in the presence of unforeseen difficulties. Above all, the question of *how* you can consistently motivate individual employees is essential for day-to-day work. However, the arts of leading groups effectively, negotiating successfully, and adapting your leadership style to the maturity level of each employee are also crucial leadership skills (*on page 67*).

As the **Empathetic Psychologist**, you're aware of the different personality types and approach each employee empathetically according to their character. In this section, you will learn the essentials about various types of people and how to find common ground even with difficult employees. Employee performance reviews are the key to connecting with your employee, so learning how to conduct them successfully ensures your success. And you can't forget about team building—both when hiring new employees and within the existing team, your goal is to ensure that employees see themselves as a team and work together as one (*on page 115*).

As the **Skilled Problem Solver**, you resolve any conflicts within your team and are responsible for change management. Because necessary and sometimes unpopular decisions must be implemented in the interests of an organization, your success as a leader depends on your ability to manage conflicts and initiate necessary changes. The problem-solving tools presented in this section will help you fulfill this role with professionalism (*starting on page 139*).

Mastering these five roles is, of course, a big challenge. But believe me: You definitely want to take it on, because becoming an ideal leader will bring you inner fulfillment and continuously better feedback from employees and customers. By setting off on the path to mastering the five roles of a leader, you commit yourself to constant improvement.

This concise and easy to understand book is designed to teach you the best tools for mastering the five roles of leadership in just a few hours. You won't find any pseudo-scientific banter or endless footnotes here; we get right down to business, starting with talking about the five leadership roles in more detail.

The Five Roles of a Successful Leader

The first and most important role of a leader is the Convincing Communicator. It's true for every manager: communication is not everything, but without communication, there's nothing. For most of the day, managers are busy communicating with employees, customers, their own bosses, by phone, email, face-to-face, and in video conferences. Being able to communicate successfully is obviously invaluable, and it's no secret that not all managers have tapped into their communication potential. This chapter therefore goes over some special rhetorical tips for helping you better manage your everyday communication.

Rhetoric for Managers

Chapter overview:

01. Arguments are SEXI
02. Talking is silver—listening is gold
03. Body language is king
04. The voice sets the mood
05. Creating an open feedback culture
06. Clearly communicating values and visions

01 Arguments are SEXI

Managers are supposed to be naturally convincing. But what is the best way to convince someone of something? With a convincing argument, of course. Yet most people are not actually familiar with the elements that make up a persuasive argument. The first tool I would like to introduce is called the *SEXI model*. With this model, you can improve your argumentation skills and convince your colleagues and customers faster in just four steps.

Statement

Explanation

eXample

Impact

a) First stage of the argument: The Statement

Every good persuasion process begins with a thesis, what we call the statement. With a statement, your employee or customer gets to know the starting point of your thought process. It's a good idea to formulate your statement as clearly and concisely as possible at the beginning of a conversation. Nothing too fancy, in other words, because your audience simply doesn't have time to listen to a long story. No matter the role or position, everybody has crowded schedules these days (we'll get to the topic of efficient to-do lists in the Techniques for Efficiency and Effectiveness section). And even without the added pressure and stress of a deadline, people just like to be informed right away.

b) Second stage of the argument: The Explanation

This second stage of the argument follows immediately after the statement. The explanation gives reasons for why the statement is correct. In my 15+ years of being a coach, I've noticed that this second stage of argumentation is the most difficult one to master for most managers. Their explanations are often only two or three sentences long. This is problematic because many facts in everyday life are anything but clear and unambiguous. We therefore have to put greater effort into convincing the other person of a new idea.

And yet, it's relatively easy to see why many of us have incomplete and inadequate skills when it comes to explaining things. After all, we ourselves think that what we are proposing as a statement is a pretty good idea already. But what we forget is that, for the other person, this is usually an entirely new idea. They need good reasons to accept the statement favorably.

You see, ever since childhood, we've all had a strong need for explanation. As children, we were constantly asking why, why, and why, and rightfully so. Today, we still want to understand exactly why something happens one way and not the other. For example, if you as a manager decide that there will be no remote work in your organization or department from now on, then your employees are going to immediately ask: *"Whyyyyyy???"*

You need to provide a good explanation. This is where most managers make the following mistake. Instead of sticking to one kind of justification and elaborating on it really well, they bundle together a bunch of justifications without going into depth with any of them. The explanation ends up sounding something like this:

Dear employees,

since a few of you have been raising the topic of working from home again, I would like to comment on it directly. Employees in our department will no longer be working from home because maintaining constant contact with colleagues is not guaranteed, teams are drifting apart, and we are unable to verify actual working hours. Moreover, eliminating remote work is also in your best interest because it allows you to better separate work and personal life. Studies have also shown that working from home can lead to sleep disorders. Given these reasons, I hope you understand.

Do you notice anything? The manager didn't even begin to explain any of his five justifications for eliminating remote work. He merely listed them off. An explanation like this convinces (pretty much) no one. It would have been much better instead to explain one or several of these justification points in detail, which would make his overall explanation that much more convincing. My *10-sentence rule* has proven effective for these kinds of situations: If you have a justification for your statement, explain it in about ten sentences. For example, the point stating that "maintaining constant contact with colleagues is not guaranteed" definitely requires explanation. Why is contact not guaranteed? What exactly is preventing constant contact? How does a lack of constant contact affect internal processes in the department? What specific, concrete damage might result from this? These and other questions should be explained in the ten sentences.

So, if you put a reasonable effort into explaining individual justifications in more detail, your persuasive power will increase immensely, and you won't need to keep explaining things. The Ancient Romans had already figured this out, by the way: *argumenta ponderantur, non numerantur* – arguments are not counted, but weighed!

c) Third stage of the argument: The example

The third stage of the argument is the example that illustrates reasoning. I do not need to explain what examples are. **Good** examples, however, are: (a) verifiable; (b) easy to understand; and (c) generally well-known to all.

By *verifiable* I mean there is evidence that this specific example did in fact occur. The good example should be *easy to understand* because too much complexity tends to confuse rather than enlighten the audience. And *generally well-known to all* means that an obscure example from Papua New Guinea builds less emotional connection with the audience than, say, a familiar example from a competitor in the same city. You should also plan five to ten sentences for the example so you're able to present it in an easy-to-follow manner.

d) Fourth stage of the argument: The Impact

The fourth and final stage of the argument, the impact, has to do with relevance/importance. This stage is about showing why the argument is relevant to your staff or the customer. Ideally, you should be making references to the general, everyday importance of the topic, its usefulness to the audience in getting them to do this or refrain from doing that.

If you forget this fourth step, you may convince people of your argument's rationality, but they will probably just wave it off afterwards and simply say: "So what? Why do I care about what that guy standing up there just said? It doesn't affect me after all!" And this is exactly what this fourth stage of argumentation is about: Your listener should realize that what you're saying indeed affects him and his (work) life directly, so he should get busy changing his thinking or behavior. In short: You convince with the first three stages of the argument, and animate with the fourth.

EXERCISE #1: The imaginary speech

Using the SEXI model, prepare a speech explaining to your staff in detail why there will be no more remote work at your organization (speech length: approx. 3 – 5 min.). After completing your speech, please do a little research on the Internet and find some good reasons for not having employees work from home. With this in mind, analyze the speech you gave: Did your speech give the best reasons? Were the reasons sufficiently explained and justified? Did you provide a good example? Did you make the topic relevant to your audience? If you have to announce a big decision soon, remember the SEXI model and apply it consistently from now on.

02 Talking is silver—listening is gold

Persuasion is one of the most important skills of a good leader, of course. But what about listening? How important of a skill is listening? And are there different ways of listening? To get right to the point: Yes, there are actually seven ways to listen . A seemingly mundane, everyday activity is actually more complex than we thought. Let's take a closer look at the seven ways of listening:

7 Ways of Listening

a) Empathetic listening

At the top of the list is empathetic listening. It's a sincere attempt to not only understand what your conversation partner is saying, but also get a good feel of what drives him in the first place. Knowing this, then, allows you to help him.

Example: When your employee tells you, his manager, about a dispute with his colleague, you not only understand what the background of the dispute was, but you also empathize completely with your employee's position, listening to him long enough to then give him a concrete suggestion for a solution. You do not avoid the situation. Instead, you create a relaxed and familiar atmosphere and focus 100% of your attention on your employee. The goal of the highest level of listening is to genuinely help the other person.

b) Active listening

Active listening is an honest and active attempt to understand the other person. It's a matter of paraphrasing what has been said, and asking questions to make sure you have really understood what has been said. That way, you avoid misunderstandings.

Example: Your employee tells you about a dispute with his colleague. You try to fully understand the employee by actively asking what the background of the dispute was. You ask specific questions about information the employee might have omitted; you leave no stone unturned, even if the employee preferred leaving something unsaid (unconsciously or not). Thus the second highest level of listening is about understanding the other person one hundred percent.

c) Attentive listening

Attentive listening is a rather passive attempt at understanding what the other person is talking about. At this level, you listen attentively but make no effort to actively seek out information and clear up any ambiguities by asking specific questions.

Example: When your employee tells you about an argument he had with a colleague, you, as the manager, try not to miss any information. After the employee has finished, you assess the situation without investigating further. This third highest level of listening is about understanding the other person for the most part.

d) Interruptive listening

At this listening level, we listen to the other person but interrupt him when we feel that the specific information is rather unimportant, thus limiting his flow of speech.

Example: Your employee tells you that making a new website for your company would be a good idea. You know, however, that he's no senior designer, but an industrial engineer, so he wouldn't have the competence to comment on this matter anyway. You therefore interrupt him, frequently looking at the clock because you have another appointment soon. Before long, you're already making your way towards the door—a clear signal to the employee that the conversation should be wrapping up now. This fourth highest level of listening is about generally understanding the other person.

e) Projective listening

At this level, you're not listening to the other person completely, but sporadically. You only pick up key phrases while the rest is overheard or overlaid by your own thoughts. In your head you latch onto these key phrases and add what the other person probably wanted to say.

Example: Your employee tells you he's working a lot of overtime on a current project and that he quite likes the project—as long as he has nothing to do with the client directly. You're expecting the employee to complain about the overtime, so you single out the buzzwords "overtime" and "nothing to do with the client." In your head, you interpret this as the employee not finding anything positive about the project. You completely miss the fact that he indeed likes the project for the most part. This fifth stage of listening is about understanding the other person selectively and only to a certain extent, your own thoughts clearly taking precedence in the conversation.

f) Pretending listening

At this level, we look at the other person but don't actually listen. Instead, we just pretend that the person has our full attention.

Example: You're on the phone talking to your employee about a project timeline—but in reality, you're thinking about a mediocre sales call you had with a potential customer ten minutes ago, where you made a few mistakes. The employee's info on the timeline seems unimportant to you, so you just mutter the occasional "Mhhh ..." and "Aha ..." but you're not reflecting on what he's actually saying. This sixth level of listening is about making the other person feel like you're listening when in fact you're not listening at all.

g) Ignoring listening

Although you're hearing what the other person is saying, you're not paying any attention to the content. The other person talking is more like a distracting background noise. You don't even bother to catch anything specific.

Example: Your assistant comes into your office for a moment and speaks to you, but you're busy writing an important email and want to word it perfectly. Not once does your focus leave the screen. But it doesn't matter: In ten minutes you'll forget that your assistant was even there at all, let alone that he was trying to tell you something important. This seventh level of listening is about letting the other person talk, but indirectly signaling that you're not really listening to him at all.

Listening is a multi-faceted phenomenon, and everyone has experienced these seven types of listening at some point. However, the distinctions clearly show that empathetic listening and active listening take energy and time. So naturally you ask: is it even worth spending that kind of energy and time? The "seven levels of hierarchy" thought experiment can be a great help here.

h) The "seven levels of hierarchy" thought experiment

Imagine you're a manager with six levels of hierarchy below you. You form the top (seventh) level. Now, imagine that at each level down the hierarchy, 50% of relevant information is lost due to careless listening. So, on the first level there is 100% of information, on the second level there is only 50%, and it keeps dividing in half from there. How much information do you think is left for you at the top (seventh) level? Got a number in mind? The answer: only 1.6% of the original 100% of info gets to you at the top (seventh) level! This thought experiment comes from a colleague of mine, Thomas Zweifel. Here's a graph to illustrate it:

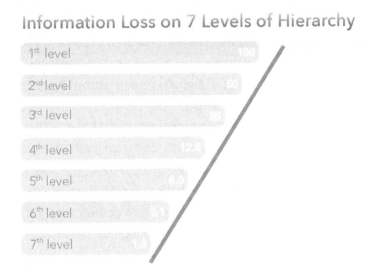

The graph clearly shows one thing: the higher the manager is on the hierarchy (up to level seven), the more important active and empathetic listening skills become in order to get the full story, 100% of the info. What's also clear is this: If the manager wants access to more relevant information, he must go to the "source", i.e., pose direct questions to the first or second level as well. Only having "strategy sessions" in the board room is just not enough. After all, who can make a sound decision with merely 1.6% of the info behind it?! Hence the saying: Talking is silver—listening is gold.

EXERCISE #2: Listen to a TED Talk

Listen to a TED Talk without taking any notes (www.ted.com). If you don't know which TED Talk, I recommend the one by Simon Sinek titled "How great leaders inspire action" (just enter it on YouTube). TED Talks, if you're not familiar with them, are approx. 20-minute-long presentations by various leaders in their respective fields with great ideas for the world.

And now for your task: Listen to the talk and, afterward, take pen and paper and write down as many details as possible. Then listen to the talk again. Did you remember all the major points? What about the examples? Did you note down the presenter's justifications? The beauty of this listening exercise is that you can easily check your skills and train yourself to listen carefully without needing any extra coaching, as there are hundreds of good TED Talks to check out. Added bonus: You'll greatly improve your listening skills while getting plenty of clever ideas—and not just for your working life.

03 Body language is king

Thousands of books have been written on professional body language. I myself regularly hold two-day events with managers on perfecting their body language. But this book isn't just for show. It's a practical manual, and let me tell you, you can improve 80% of the effect you have on others (keyword: Pareto principle) if you practice these three body language tips:

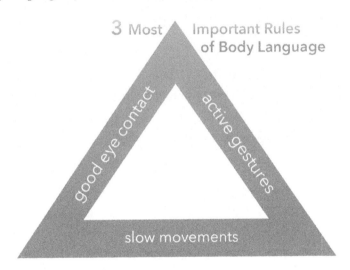

a) Why is eye contact so important?

The first body language rule is about eye contact. Eye contact builds trust, suggests competence, and radiates self-confidence. But the most important reason is that eye contact allows us to observe exactly how the other person is receiving our message. Whether the other person is looking away, embarrassed, frowning, or even shaking his head—we can observe the smallest body language reactions with eye contact and adapt our speech accordingly.

I've been one of the most successful speakers in various rhetoric competitions and world debating championships, but it was only partly due to my powers of persuasion. More importantly, I kept a close eye on the jury evaluating my speeches and noticed exactly when they had "swallowed" my argument. If the juror frowned at the first part of my argument, it did me no good to continue along with the second part. I had to better explain the first part of argument, perhaps explain it differently or give another example. Only when the juror nodded and wrote something on his paper did I know for sure that I could continue with the second part.

And that same rule applies to everyday life: if you notice in a staff review, for example, that your employee simply isn't following what you're saying, then you need to try it from a different perspective or with different reasoning. While doing so, maintain constant eye contact and analyze his body language for approval and disapproval.

The good thing about body language is that most people are bad actors in this regard. They can't control their body language that easily. Thus the body "speaks" the truth without the speaker ever actually vocalizing it. The famous Mehrabian study from 1967 states that people intuitively know the truthfulness of body language. They'd sooner believe body language than spoken language. So, if a person says that he is looking forward to the Christmas party (verbal level), but he's looking down, a little embarrassed while saying it (non-verbal level), you might be more inclined to believe his body language, and would probably be right. Body language reveals what the spoken word might otherwise try to hide. If you're interested in the art of manipulation, I recommend my book *Dark Rhetoric: Manipulate Before You're Manipulated!*.

Since you're now in a leadership position in your organization, you'll be making small speeches, taking charge of meetings, and giving presentations more frequently. This also means that your body language will be under much more scrutiny than before. But don't panic! It's actually a great opportunity. In the spirit of Winston Churchill:

> „A pessimist sees a difficulty in every opportunity;
> an optimist sees an opportunity in every difficulty."

Being a leader and having to work on your own body language is a heavy burden indeed. But it's also a chance to increase your overall effectiveness in giving speeches. Good body language combined with a good speech gets your message across to your staff that much quicker. Think of it as a big challenge with a big reward!

b) Gestures emphasize content

Now for the second fundamental body language rule: spoken language should be emphasized with physical gestures. That way, the listener can better remember what was said. The problem: many people don't use their hands at all when speaking. They either just hang there stiff and lifeless, are cramped up for almost the entire speech, or they're fiddling around with a pen or a ring – which comes off as being very nervous.

But even small, purposeful gestures can have a great effect. You must be wondering which gestures fit when? How often should you gesture? When is it too much?

These are all valid questions. But I'll let you in on the most important gesture tool right away: your very own gesture vocabulary. What is that, exactly? Very simple: You can come up with your own gestures for frequently recurring words and concepts that fit your speech's content. And that's the beauty of the physical gesture. There is no right or wrong, neither too much nor too little. There should only be a few appropriate hand movements after all, gestures which clarify content. Here are some examples:

- *If you have multiple points in your speech, count through those points on your fingers.*

- *When you weigh something, make a movement with your hands like a scale.*

- *If you want to specify something, then draw a dot in the air.*

- *If you want the audience to pay attention, raise your index finger.*

So, to put it simply: give your thought an accompanying gesture. What is said is then not only heard, but seen, increasing the overall effectiveness of your speech. Of course, your gesture vocabulary is rather small at the beginning. But it can be easily expanded. If you see other people using interesting and appealing gestures, try them yourself at home. Add a little something to make them your own.

One thing is clear: a person with expressive gestures not only appears but really feels more confident and knowledgeable. It definitely pays to invest in your own gestures.

c) Slow movements exude calm

One of the most common problems leaders face is stage fright. You're in the spotlight a lot and have a lot of eyes staring at you. Some managers avoid this situation in front of an audience as if their lives depended on it. The result: a lot of nervousness in the body, which translates into too much movement. For some, it's the "dancing back and forth" with the feet; for others, the nervous "looking here and there" with the eyes, or even flinching with the entire upper body.

If jerky movements make you feel uncomfortable, they definitely make you look uncomfortable. And what's more: many equate shaky, sketchy body language with shaky, sketchy content. The listener is thinking: "That guy up there sure seems uncomfortable. Maybe he's uncomfortable with what he's saying too?"

This makes it all the more important to train yourself to use body language slowly and consciously. I therefore invite you to do the following exercise.

EXERCISE #3: The homemade video

Do a completely spontaneous 3-minute speech on the topic, "is work-life balance a myth?" Record this speech with your smartphone or with your laptop camera. The "send video message" function on Skype also works well. You should be visible down to the waist. After you're done, watch your recording without sound. That way, you can better focus on your body language during the analysis.

Questions for self-analysis: Did you maintain constant eye contact with the camera? Make a few gestures? Were you moving slowly? Did you make awkward gestures, such as touching your face?

An extra tip: if you're not satisfied with the first one, make a second recording, a third. Practice makes perfect, even with body language.

04 The voice sets the mood

Your voice sets the tone of what you are saying. Many people don't realize that a vocal melody and a mood are carried along in every spoken sentence, coloring the words in a very specific way.

As a manager, you're the one that's ultimately responsible for setting the mood or atmosphere in your department. Even if you're just giving daily instructions, managing or controlling your own voice can set the tone for the rest of the workday. Here are the essential dimensions of voice that are within your power to control.

a) Enthusiasm

Imagine you're giving a short speech to your staff. Does your voice sound alive? Is it full of movement, vitality? Or is it rather calm sounding, even cautious or strictly businesslike? As a coach, I train both young and experienced managers to speak enthusiastically almost everyday.

What's the problem I see with most of them? Managers often work more than everyone else, which can lead to chronic fatigue and exhaustion. But how are you supposed to sound full of life when you're dead tired all the time?

True, workload and tone of voice are directly correlated for most people. But "doing a lot" doesn't always have to mean "getting a lot done." You just have to increase your productivity – more on this in the next chapter, "Techniques for Efficiency and Effectiveness." But first, let's do a status-quo analysis of the voice.

You don't have to be a voice expert or an opera singer to hear the mood that is being conveyed when you speak. You can perform your own voice coaching session with the following exercise.

EXERCISE #4: The homemade sound recording

Imagine you have a new employee and you want to give him a brief one-on-one about the current responsibilities of your department. You also have to briefly introduce yourself, of course. Make up a short speech for this purpose (duration: 2–3 min.). You can use the voice recorder of your smartphone to capture it. A voice recording program is usually pre-installed. If you can't find it, just download a free audio recording app. It'll take you 30 seconds to get things ready.

Make your recording, then listen to it and analyze it with the following questions: Do you talk with enthusiasm? Is the tone of your voice pleasant and motivating? Are you talking too fast? Too slow? Do you emphasize important information? And don't forget: Do you like listening to yourself? Or do you feel like stopping the recording because it all sounds a bit tired and drawn out?

If the latter is the case, don't worry. Just try it again. For most people, the second recording is already much better than the first, because you become aware of the off-putting mood in your voice and work to change it. If you don't want to give your own speeches, feel free to read an editorial from the Washington Post or New York Times aloud for the recording. Pay attention to how you lead your voice throughout it. In the end, achieving a genuinely enthusiastic tone of voice is a lot like jogging: the more you do it, the better you get.

And one last note: Even if you don't feel like you're in a perfect mood or full of energy, try to speak with as much enthusiasm as you can anyway. After all, you'll no doubt face situations where you simply have to grind through the day with a smile on your face, even though your real mood might sooner scare off the customer or team. But if you at least sound enthusiastic, this creates a positive feedback of good moods: the more positive you sound, the more positive your team reacts, which in turn makes you feel more positive.

b) Correct emphasis

It's amazing how much a change in emphasis can alter the meaning of a sentence. Take, for example, the three emphasis variations of the following sentence. When you read it , emphasize the highlighted word in each variation:

Correct Emphasis

1. **Our** department believes it could work.

2. Our department **believes** it could work.

3. Our department believes it **could** work.

On the surface, the four variations are identical. But because of the different emphasis, each variation has a completely different focus. **In sentence 1**, you emphasize that your department in particular (as distinct from other departments) believes it can work. **In sentence 2**, the emphasis is on the word "believes." Here, the speaker can say the word enthusiastically, emphasizing that the department doesn't know for sure but is still convinced that it could work. A skeptical emphasis on the word "believes," though, focuses on the fact that the department isn't really convinced that it could work. **In sentence 3**, you emphasize the word "could," thus highlighting the word's subjunctive nature (i.e., the possibility of something working or not working). Here, the listener will think: "Could work. Could also not work!"

And this sentence is no special exception. A potential shift in meaning through emphasis exists in every sentence we speak in everyday life. As a leader, you should therefore always consciously consider what your main message should be. Depending on what it is, you then place the emphasis in your sentences accordingly.

c) Conscious pausing

You've of course heard that pauses are important when speaking. This is nothing new. But how many people do you think use deliberate pauses when they talk? Is it 50% of speakers? 20%? My experience is: less than 10%.

How can it be that everyone knows how important making pauses in their speech is, but hardly anyone takes them? In reality, most people have read this somewhere at some point in time but are not exactly clear on *why* they should be using pauses. So they just leave them out instead.

There are three good reasons for rhetorical pauses: First, a leader who takes deliberate pauses comes across as much more confident. A leader rattling through his content as quickly as possible: not so much. Second, the pause gives the audience time to reflect on what has been said. This is because employees are hearing the content for the first time and need time to digest the information. Third, the pause gives employees a chance to ask or add something.

And the latter is probably a secret reason why the pause is dreaded by so many people. Indeed, the fear of questions and criticism leads many to prefer not to take any pauses at all. That way, nothing can be added nor criticized. And that doesn't just apply to managers. Many university professors talk their way through the entire lecture without allowing so much as a single question. I don't even need to mention politicians and their quick disappearances after their statements at press conferences.

But it's precisely the opportunity to ask questions or contribute one's thoughts that creates an open communication culture in your organization! All you need to do is pause. So the next time you're sharing something with your employees at a meeting, take a deliberate pause after a part of your speech and look around questioningly. Maybe someone has a valuable addition or an even better idea to add. Don't forget to make it very clear to your employees that you're happy to hear all ideas, agreeing or otherwise. More on open communication culture is coming up in the next chapter.

If you would like to have even more communication tips, I recommend my online course "20 Best Communication Hacks: Influence and Persuade People".

05 Creating an open feedback culture

So why is the open feedback culture especially beneficial for you as a manager? It's obvious: open feedback gives you more information and the opportunity to choose from a wider pool of ideas. At the same time – and this is the second major advantage – an open communication culture is more fun for your employees because they can actively contribute in the workplace. It also shows them that you value their viewpoints.

So, if an open communication and feedback culture is such a great thing, why isn't it practiced in every company? The cause is usually the affected manager himself. Let's imagine three everyday scenarios that affect an open feedback culture.

Scenario 1: The manager knows more than the employees. A few brave people from the company speak out, but their ideas are constantly pushed back and rebuffed by the "superior" manager. At the same time, the leader is enjoying his alpha status. Yet over time, even the more vocal and courageous employees quit trying to speak up. They simply don't want to fight against such strongly opinionated behavior anymore.

Scenario 2: The manager knows less than the employees. It's often the case here that the manager gets scared about losing his position. Better ideas are the worst thing that can happen, because not being the best feels like you don't deserve the top position. Maybe your employees are chipping away at you and your job with their great ideas. So clearly, in this scenario it's not bossiness but fear that prevents the open communication culture from developing.

Scenario 3: The manager criticizes a lot and never praises. Making new and creative suggestions in this scenario is simply unreasonable from the perspective of any reasonable employee. Because if the boss doesn't like the idea, the employee will be criticized for it. And if it's a great idea, the employee won't get any credit for it anyway. So why bother? It's more sensible to just stay quiet and simply meet the target.

These three scenarios hinder open feedback culture the most. Especially during in-house training sessions, I notice that – as soon as the boss walks in the room – the employees hardly participate anymore. They suddenly become quiet as mice. When their manager is present at my Impulse Talk, the employees in the audience are often very hesitant to respond to my questions. Their mindset is obvious: as an employee, I could embarrass myself in front of the boss, so why take the risk?

And what applies to training courses and lectures therefore naturally applies to your meetings. As an employee, why risk my head? Why contradict my boss? Why not just keep a low profile?

But as a result of this negative behavior, problems and ideas are not put on the table, and things that need to change simply don't.

So, what can you do about it?

I recommend you take the following four strategies to heart in order to quickly and credibly create an open feedback culture in your organization:

a) "Opposition is welcome!"

The first strategy is to emphasize that you value opposing views in meetings and discussions of all kinds. Not only among employees, but also with you. And if you are actually contradicted, please don't fall into the justification trap and explain why you are actually right after all. You won't come across as credible if you ask for opposition but then decide that you know better about everything. Let better ideas convince you.

And more importantly: admit it when an employee has a better idea or a good point of criticism. Even if it feels a little uncomfortable at first, think pragmatically. You get a valuable correction, and this benefits the entire department.

b) "Give credit where credit is due."

When I ask my coaching clients if they get praise from their bosses, the most common response is: *"I wish!"* And that, of course, is a shame. Many managers are perfectionists. They feel that not reprimanding is praise enough. I cannot recall getting a single moment of praise from my supervisor from previous jobs in law firms and during my time at the United Nations in New York. The boss that never praises is definitely an international phenomenon.

But keep in mind, praise makes everyone happy. Praise is direct feedback, even with a simple: "Keep up the good work!" And finally, praise is motivating. All super reasons to praise your staff. But why aren't employees getting showered with praise, then?

The answer: we live in a "praise-less" society, so it's hard to try to change the culture and be the first one to give praise. Unconsciously, most think, *"I didn't get any praise – so why should I give it?"*

And of course there's something to that. If you yourself have never been praised, you are stingy. You can easily compare it with money: those with little of it probably won't donate it to others.

But the reasons given for praising employees are overwhelming. Especially in the context of the open feedback culture, when you praise someone, a "thank you" will circle back to you in the form of new, good ideas. Praise improves both mood and output. So, what are you waiting for? Get over yourself and praise where appropriate!

c) "Deliver criticism with care."

Of course, you don't want your organization or department to be drowned in praise, as if it were perfect and absolutely flawless. Criticism is necessary. But you should definitely consider the manner in which you deliver criticism. The rhetorical motto has existed since antiquity: **Hard on the problem, soft on the people!**

It means you shouldn't leave out anything factual in your criticism, and you should criticize duly. But, the criticism should not be personal. Here are a few examples:

Example 1: Instead of, *"You did that all wrong!"*, you might say, *"The way you did it was not optimal because XYZ. For the future, please try it in the following way ..."* With this last one, you're giving the employee precise instructions and gently reminding him of his mistake without condemning him.

Example 2: Instead of, *"You've made that mistake before!"*, you might say, *"Do you remember that we had a similar case some time ago and agreed that you would do so and so?"* Here, you're reminding the employee of a past conversation. Wait for his reaction. Maybe he has reasons why he deviated from it.

Example 3: Instead of, *"You've gotten pretty slow at your work – what's going on?"*, you might say, *"I've noticed that you're doing the work a little slower than you used to. How can I help you get back to performing as well as you did before?"* This is where you offer direct help to the employee. It's not pure altruism, of course. It's a goal-oriented attempt to return the employee to his former, better performance level. Also note that this is an open-ended question that asks the employee to say more than just a simple yes or no.

EXERCISE #5: Becoming more diplomatic

Take note of where you have been too harsh with your criticism in the past. Phrase your criticism more diplomatically. Note down, too, where you could have praised an employee or colleague but did not. Finally, think about situations where you were criticized and how you felt about it. Write it down. These three examples will help you become aware of the existing communication culture in your organization. Along with the other tips from this chapter, the examples will help steer that culture in a more positive direction.

06 Clearly communicate your organization's values and vision

Every company has values and visions. But it's often the case that they're only known to management, not the employees. There are even companies that have not worked out their values and visions at all.

What's clear, however, is that values and visions give both managers and employees orientation and a sense of purpose for going to work. Everyone who works ends up asking the question: *"Why am I doing what I'm doing?"* And if you don't get a satisfactory answer to that, you then ask *"Why am I working for this organization?"*

Especially in the 21st century, there's an ever-increasing thirst among employees to know what exactly they're investing their lives in when they work eight hours a day, every day. Just think of "Generation Y" here. A clear, normative positioning of the company is therefore extremely important for employee retention.

a) Define your organization's values and vision.

If your organization already has a "mission statement"—great! If not, you should work one out with the leadership team. A mission statement ensures that the organization is sailing in a well-defined direction. Perhaps you know the saying,

> „If a man knows not what port he sails, no wind is favorable."

and this also applies to companies: If there's no overarching goal, then profit maximization will be all that's left eventually. And that would be quite a shame.

A little challenge for you: Let's assume you're the European head of booking.com. What would your mission statement be? Write down one or two sentences. Set the book aside for a minute and write it down on a piece of paper. Don't read the next paragraph until you're done.

A possible mission statement could definitely be: "You'll find the best/ cheapest hotels with us." But the real mission statement sounds much better: *"Our mission is to make it easier for everyone to experience the world."* It's very appealing to customers. But it's also very motivating for employees because they feel part of an organization that's connecting people to travel opportunities they wouldn't otherwise have.

Ideally, a vision is simple and understandable for all employees. An example from Amazon CEO Jeff Bezos drives the point home. His vision for Amazon is simple: *"Low prices, fast delivery, vast selection."*

Simple, but ingenious. It's a vision completely independent of time and technology. No matter what the world will look like in 30 years, people will always want the lowest possible prices for products delivered quickly and from a huge selection.

b) Exemplify values and vision as a leader of your organization.

To be credible, of course, the organization's values must also be exemplified in daily life, especially by managers. Google did it perfectly in 2017 when one of their employees claimed that women are biologically less suited for the tech industry. Google responded by handing said employee his resignation. It's simple: the employee had disregarded his organization's core values, so management acted quickly and fired him on the spot. Google was sending a clear signal to women in the tech world, making their values clear to the entire world in the process.

The Google example represents open communication culture: Anyone who preaches values but never allows himself to be criticized is certainly not being a good leader; rather, he's being entirely counterproductive to the proclaimed values. A good leader is not guided by status but by the better argument. And, of course, if an employee has the better rationale or evidence, a good leader praises him, acknowledging his point immediately. In US organizations, people often talk about the *"power of proof"*: He who has the proof is right.

The message is clear: if a manager preaches about water but drinks wine, he appears untrustworthy. Words should always be consistent with actions, no matter the values and vision you've defined.

c) Consolidate values and vision.

Defining and exemplifying are not everything, of course. Every good manager will enter into dialog with employees, discuss these values and visions, find examples of how individual employees have achieved the organization's goals with the help of these values, celebrate these stories in a newsletter or via intranet, for example, and hold training sessions and team events in which the values and vision are made the central topic. During recruiting, a good manager will also ensure that applicants are not only fit for the job on paper, but that they exhibit a professionalism in line with the organization's values, too. And likewise, employees who disregard the organization's values and visions are simply kept away or – as in Google's example—terminated.

Another good example is the company Trivago, which truly lives an open feedback culture. For their managers, that means responding to any and all feedback from employees. Every employee feels heard—and if the manager doesn't quite understand the feedback, he naturally follows up and asks for more information. This is the best way to consolidate your organization's values and vision into an open communication culture. After all, team events are all well and good, but integrating values and visions into everyday working life? Now that's the supreme discipline.

EXERCISE #6: Your own mission statement

Formulate a mission statement. Stuck? Get inspired by examples from the Internet. Even if your organization already has a mission statement, articulate the core values and central vision for your department specifically. Write it down. Review what actions you could take to make those goals more widely known and reinforced among your employees.

Productivity Techniques & Time Management

Chapter overview:

As a manager, you're in charge of a larger variety of tasks than, say, a specialist, who focuses on something particular. So, your success depends on how well you manage your time and your tasks. This is critical.

As a business coach, I deal with managers on a daily basis. I ask them to show me their typical work week (their schedule) when topics of productivity and effectiveness are on the agenda. You know what I've learned? I notice again and again that it's not the manager who runs everyday life, but everyday life that runs the manager.

Typical examples are overcrowded work days with little to no time for strategic thinking. There are no blocked work phases for *deep work* (high-concentration work without any disruptions). There's also a general lack of clarity about their priorities as managers.

It's amazing because the managers I work with are already familiar with the techniques for efficiency and effectiveness, but they aren't using them in their everyday work lives. So, to help you get more done in less time, I present to you the top ten productivity techniques and how you can incorporate them into your workday – every day.

01 The Eisenhower principle

One of the best effectiveness techniques out there is the Eisenhower principle. It's explained in many time management seminars but quickly forgotten. Here's a quick refresher. The principle assumes four types of tasks.

The Eisenhower Principle

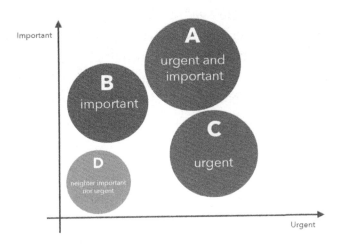

It seems simple, but the devil is in the details. The first question asks, what is actually "important?" You must define for yourself —or in cooperation with your coworkers and supervisors—what is actually important for your organization or department (the mission statement is suitable for this!).

Let's assume that new customer acquisition is currently the most important goal for you. You would have your day geared towards this goal from the very beginning. Whether cold calling, warm calling, or sales training for your team, you need to be significantly guided by the goal of customer acquisition.

In reality, of course, it's not that easy. Dozens of emails are coming in, calls and coworkers are distracting you with questions and ideas. So while the will is there to get on with the most important task, disruptions constantly get in the way. Little things like that, and lots of them, dictate your work life.

The phenomenon associated with constant distractions that extremely limit the productivity of any manager is called the **sawtooth effect**. After a disruption, it takes a certain amount of time to get back on track. The time spent getting back on track wastes valuable resources. Here is a graphic representation of the sawtooth effect:

The Swatooth Effect

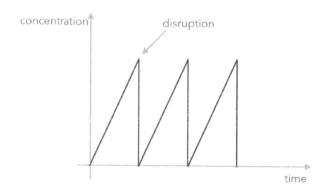

But there's a way out: Phases of *deep work* defined by you, protected times when no one is allowed to disturb you. No emails, no calls, no coworkers. Just work. These trouble-free islands of deep thought and strategic planning are paramount, especially for completing tasks in order of priority.

Robin Sharma's **90-90-1 rule** offers a great help for managers here: For 90 days, you focus the first 90 minutes of your workday on the single most important task – without any disruptive elements, of course.

Why 90 days? Because people need a certain amount of time to install a routine. After 90 days, you're automatically setting yourself up with the most important task right at the beginning.

Why 90 minutes? Well, no human being can concentrate for very long periods of time and deliver 100% of their performance every single day. From my own experience in university and at work, 90 minutes has proven to be the perfect compromise between too much work and too little time for getting into something.

Why the single most important task? People need a clear focus. Hardly anyone can concentrate on several main goals at the same time and complete them all equally well.

It's also easy to imagine yourself coming into your office in the morning, informing your colleagues that your first 90 minutes of the day are blocked, and getting down to work. If that isn't possible due to operational reasons, then set up the block period at another time. The important thing is that it should always be at the same time. That way, the habit becomes routine, and your coworkers know when they can approach you about something.

But now back to the Eisenhower principle. So, what is the difference between important and urgent tasks? And which are more crucial for our advancement?

According to the definition of the Eisenhower principle, important tasks are those that bring us closer to the goal defined in the mission statement, while urgent tasks are those that cannot be delayed. The key here is that urgent tasks only seem important because of an imminent deadline—but, they can also be left undone because they don't bring us closer to the main goal.

Studies show that most people spend 60% of their working time on C tasks. In contrast, employees at Forbes 500 companies focus mainly on B tasks; the proportion of C tasks is lower among them, too. How can you learn more from these successful companies? Follow their example: Focus more on B tasks. That's the key to the Eisenhower principle: We already do important and urgent things first even without the principle, but the principle reminds us not to get lured away by urgency, not to forget that doing C tasks is just not as important as achieving B tasks for achieving the main goal. In short: more B, less C!

Now, a quick word about D tasks. Some people need to completely check off everything on the to-do list in order to feel good about themselves. That describes the famous perfectionist trap: If I can do 100% of the tasks, then I'm working at 100% myself! Unfortunately, though, to-do lists also sneak in a lot of D tasks, such as reading through a newsletter or attending an unimportant meeting.

Sure, some tasks need to be done, even on the D list. But you should always ask yourself this question for D tasks: What happens if I don't do this task at all? And if the answer to this is "nothing, really," you should simply delete this task.

Lastly, here's a simple idea on how to integrate the Eisenhower principle into your everyday life. Take a white sheet of paper, preferably a large one, and divide it into four quadrants. Jot down planned tasks, even spontaneous ones that might come up during the day, in the appropriate quadrants. That way, you know exactly in which order you need to work through which tasks. Your sheet of paper can look something like this:

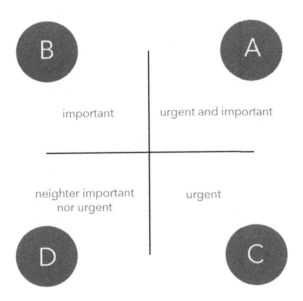

important | urgent and important

neighter important nor urgent | urgent

EXERCISE #7: 7 days of Eisenhower

Try it out for a week, right now! It's neat just how effective it is. Consciously placing a task into one of the quadrants ensures that you are actively sorting tasks by importance for achieving your overarching goal from the mission statement. This awareness and focus you're raising is exactly what increases your productivity.

02 **The not-to-do list**

The Eisenhower principle, on paper, is a glorified to-do list. Sure. But there's another ingenious idea that has become very popular among executives in the US: the not-to-do list. In order to unclutter the daily routine, the manager clearly defines what not to do.

The list will look a bit different for everyone, of course. To put it more succinctly, here's a snippet from my own not-to-do list:

MY **NOT TO DO** LIST

a) No Netflix or TV series.

b) No reading emails when going to sleep or getting up.

c) No more than three times a day for checking emails.

d) No Outlook after sending emails.

e) No online chess for longer than 30 minutes (set an alarm).

I don't check emails or read the news in bed because I want to feel positive and motivated in the morning, not have it spoiled by potentially negative messages, which would set a negative tone for the rest of the day. I deliberately keep Outlook turned off until 11:00 AM so I can focus on the main task of the day according to the 90-90-1 rule described above. After answering important emails, I close Outlook so as not to have any further distractions. I also don't watch documentary series or Netflix. They eat up my free time way too much, I find. No pouring over emails/messages in the evening either. That way, I'm not troubled by potentially negative information before going to bed, and can fall asleep quickly.

EXERCISE #8: The not-to-do list

Your own not-to-do list will look different, of course. Think about what your current big time wasters are and what bad habits you could refrain from. Print the list out and place it in a visible spot on your workstation. Over time, you'll memorize the items on the not-to-do list. You'll be more satisfied that you have more time for the essentials.

03 The ALPEN method

The ALPEN method by Lothar Seiwert is a wonderful complement to the Eisenhower principle. The technique doesn't refer to any mountains, even though *Alpen* is the German word for the alps. It's an acronym:

Always define tasks

Length estimation

Put in buffer time

Enact decisions

Never leave without checking

For the **Always define tasks** step, use the quadrants from the Eisenhower principle.

In the **Length estimation** step, you're supposed to define a realistic amount of time that you assign to a particular task. Simply write the duration in brackets. If you add up the times of the tasks written down, you get a good idea of what you can realistically accomplish that day. For example, if you only have ten hours of work time available but your plan adds up to twelve hours on paper, that's not a bad thing. You work through the tasks according to their importance, remember? It therefore doesn't matter all that much whether unimportant tasks get completed. The unimportant tasks can either be deleted or pushed to the next day.

The **Put in buffer time** step is about acknowledging that tasks and people can pop up unexpectedly. Buffer times are there as a cushion. They take into account that difficult tasks may take longer than planned (which, by the way, is not a bad thing either, as important tasks have to be completed).

The big question is: what percentage of my day should I schedule? 90 %? 80 %? It depends on the individual and how often unexpected things crop up in your organization. The general recommendation from most time management coaches is: You only need to schedule 60%. Otherwise, you end up still sitting in front of your computer at the office at 9:00 PM after scheduling your entire day, wondering: "Why am I still not finished? I planned my entire day to a T, didn't I?" Sure, you planned your tasks perfectly, but you didn't take disruptions and unexpected events into account, and these can add up quickly.

The penultimate step, **Enact decisions**, is about the actual work. After all, something has to be done in addition to all the planning.

The last step, **Never leave without checking**, is about evaluating the day. What has been completed, what's not quite done, and what may have been forgotten altogether? Conclusions should also be made in this end phase of day as a kind of plan for the next day. That way, ALPEN becomes a process of continuous improvement. This is what the Eisenhower principle, extended by the ALPEN method, might look like:

04 The Pareto principle

Surely you know the Pareto principle, which suggests you can achieve quite a lot with little effort. In precise terms, a mere 20% effort turns into an 80% yield.

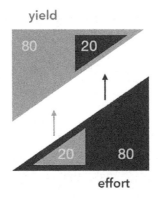

80/20 Pareto Principle

As a manager, how can you integrate the Pareto principle into your everyday work life? Well, basically you can distinguish between internal company actions (yourself and your organization), and external actions (customers and partners). Everything should be perfect on the outside, but not necessarily the inside. What I mean by that is,

suppose you are preparing an internal presentation using PowerPoint. Some managers invest hours into making the slides colorful and perfectly seamless. But we have to recognize here that for the employees, getting 80% of information retention from the slides would be absolutely sufficient. Your employees showering you with praise for your beautifully designed slides doesn't really do much, at the end of the day. The same applies to the formulating internal emails: they don't have to have perfect style. Rather, they need to be functional and get the message across.

True, some tasks need to be 100% perfectly executed in both style and content. When sending a quote to a potential client, for example—errors and inaccuracies definitely wouldn't impress them. Therefore, for each task, define what's really required to get the job done, and save on work that wouldn't have an impact.

EXERCISE #9: Pareto in your everyday work life

Make a note of tasks where perfectionism is not needed but an 80% yield would be absolutely sufficient. And be happy that you only have to put in 20% effort on these tasks!

The tip for daily implementation: When you're writing in your Eisenhower principle quadrants, just put a small *(p)* [stands for Pareto, of course] in brackets after tasks where 80% is enough to complete them. And then, when you work through the to-do list, you'll know that 20% effort is all you need, guaranteed.

05 The SMART formula

The SMART formula, another acronym, helps a manager formulate goals correctly. It stands for:

Specific

Measurable

Attractive

Realisitc

Timed

While the Eisenhower principle helps you prioritize properly, the SMART formula helps you check whether the goal is well-defined.

The goal should be specific enough that you and your team know exactly where the ship is sailing. It should be measurable so that you and the team can review how fast you are progressing, what you need to change, and when you will reach the goal. The goal should be attractive; you and your employees are naturally motivated to achieve it. It should also be realistic: Not so easy that you're done way ahead of schedule, but not so difficult that you get fed up with it. And finally, the goal should be timed, i.e., it should have a deadline.

When setting deadlines, you as a leader should follow *Parkinson's law:* work expands so as to fill the time available for its completion. Simply put, if a project is given a four-month completion date, it will take at least four months to complete it. And if a project has two months, it'll be done in two months.

EXERCISE #10: Your smart goals

Write down your annual and quarterly goals and see if they meet SMART requirements. If not, readjust.

06 Physical fitness

It may come as a bit of a surprise to see physical fitness here as a technique for efficiency and effectiveness. But, as you might have guessed, your performance is directly related to your physical energy level. The physically fit have more stamina. Above all, our sleep, food and general state of health determine our physical fitness. Now for more detail.

a) The importance of sleep

A study has shown that straight-A students lose their very good grades as soon as they consistently have too little sleep. And everybody knows that tiredness means terrible concentration.

A study of NASA pilots showed that a 26-minute nap in the afternoon improved pilot performance by 34%. So, if you can afford a nap, take it.

An experiment by Professor Jan Born, who was awarded the prestigious Leibniz Prize in 2010, also points to the importance of sleep. It showed that after getting sufficient sleep, we can solve logical tasks much better the next day. How much sleep each person needs can vary, of course. Everyone knows how much gas they need in the tank to get going. Not adhering to a consistent sleep pattern has been proven to make you less productive.

b) The importance of food

This book is not a food guide. But I would like to briefly touch on two points that affect your daily performance. First: eating your fill at lunch all but guarantees a performance slump in the afternoon, wasting an hour or two of productive work time. It's therefore better to eat less but more often, including healthy snacks such as nuts or carrots in between meals.

Second: the midday slump hits us even when we're not stuffing our bellies, so it's advisable to deliberately avoid mentally demanding tasks after lunch. For example, answering emails in the afternoon is a welcome task; it's little effort, but it has to be done. When the lull in your performance ends (around 3:00 PM), you can devote yourself to important tasks again.

c) The importance of health

As a business coach, I regularly encounter managers who say they don't have time to take care of their health. They prefer taking pills rather than addressing the root causes of their complaints. This kind of behavior is short-sighted because physical ailments can make you less efficient in the long term if left unchecked.

For example, let's say a manager has back pain. Back pain naturally shows up sooner or later in a noticeable way. It begins to distract him, meaning he can't concentrate on his work 100%. As a result, he doesn't make the best decisions and becomes less productive. The back pain might even increase, leading to even less productivity. It just makes sense in the long run to address the causes of physical complaints right away – even if it takes some time to find the right doctor. It's all in the spirit of your health and wellbeing.

EXERCISE #11: Increase your own health awareness

Keep a sleep journal for one week, noting how many hours of sleep you get. Think about what healthy snacks you could eat during small breaks at work so you don't have to fill up at lunch. Write it down. And finally, make note of any physical ailments – even the small aches and pains, because they're distracting you from work too. Actively take care of your body get a good night's sleep to become an energetic and productive leader!

07 The yes trap

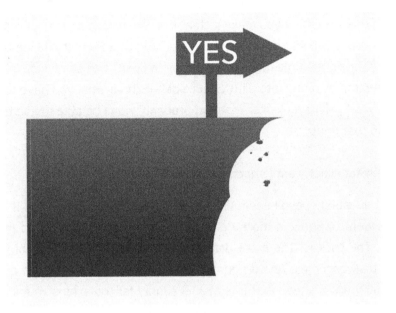

Do you have too much to do right now? Too many calls? Too many emails? You must have fallen into the yes trap some time ago. The question at some point was, "Hey, could you give me a hand with this?" You replied, "Yes," quite politely. You also said "yes" frequently in emails and phone calls. Your silent non-response was cause for many to send you more emails. And even politely stalling on the phone didn't get your conversation partners to hang up.

If this sounds like you, then it's time to say "no" more often. Here are some ways to escape the yes trap:

a) "Later, perhaps"

With this statement you make it clear that you have a lot to do already. But it's not as harsh as an absolute "No!" You could also try the phrase: "If I can find the time later, I'll be happy to do it." Add some kick to the statement by going into a little more detail about what you have to do this week. Make it clearer that you probably won't be able to find time to do that thing.

b) "What exactly am I supposed to be doing here?"

This question doesn't seem like much at first glance. You act as if you just want to know in more detail what the other person wants from you. The trick is: The more detail the other person gives, the bigger the task becomes. And if you ask once or twice more, you can quite confidently conclude that this task is simply far too extensive for you to take on at the moment. Then, you politely refuse them.

c) "Now is unfortunately not the best time"

This one's a classic from the hundred polite alternatives to "no." Again, as with point a), you can't do the assigned task because you're already swamped with other projects. However, you can also kick this one up a notch by emphasizing the word "unfortunately," pretending you're sorry it didn't work out – if only you had time. It might come off as dishonest, but then again the other person won't be interested in pressing further, because really, you'd love to if you could ...

d) Offer something different

The point here is to make a counter-proposal according to the motto: "I can't offer you X, but I'd be happy to offer you Y." Y is not so labor-intensive for you and, in order for the other person to accept the alternative suggestion, it should have some benefit for him.

e) "No"

There's always the pure and simple "no," with or without justification. With a "no," you're clearly conveying to the other person that the task can't be completed "just like that". Of course you can always word it with, "No, I wouldn't like to do that job for you," spoken in a calm manner and with zero animosity.

Giving a flat-out "no" might cost you sympathy points with the other person, but it gains you time to work on what's most important. An apt quote about this: *"Everybody is somebody's fool."* And above all, as a manager, you can't afford to be the fool. You need time, time for strategic thinking, customer contact, meetings, this, that, and the other thing. It's far better for you to just say "no" once in awhile, give up a few sympathy points, but gain more time for your tasks and yourself.

EXERCISE #12: Say "no" more often

Think about when you said "yes" in the last four weeks and regretted it afterwards. In doing so, consider the reasons that led you to agree. Write them down. This analysis will help you better understand your own inner mechanisms, allowing you to confidently say "no" more often.

08 The blocking method

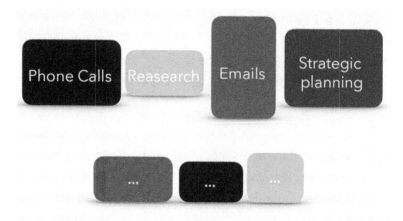

The blocking method (a.k.a. the *time* blocking method) states that similar tasks should be completed in a single block of time. This is true for telephone calls, emails, or strategy sessions, among others. The idea behind it is that you get used to similar tasks and get into a rhythm or flow, completing the tasks with ease.

If you have eight phone calls ahead of you in a day, tell the person you're talking to that if he needs a follow-up email (for example), you'll get it to him "later today." That way, you can continue working through your calls. If you jump on email writing in the middle of your calls, two things could happen: *a) You get distracted by incoming emails and answer them,* or *b) You end up taking on other tasks in order not to have to continue calling.* It's true: many people don't like to talk on the phone. The result is that telephone calls tend to be pushed back unless they're absolutely necessary. They're much more valuable for sales, for example, though the occasional phone call is still a welcome change to cold, boring emails.

So, how long the blocks should be depends on you and your task distribution (if you can get a lot done with a phone call instead of an email, for example). Someone who takes the blocking method quite seriously, by the way, is Bill Gates. He is known to take a *think week* once a year, where he reflects on long-term strategic decisions. You see? The blocking method certainly hasn't done Bill Gates any harm. Keep it in mind and try it out!

09 The salami technique

The Salami Technique

The salami technique (a.k.a. the salami-slice strategy) is based on the idea of dividing large tasks into "small slices." Sometimes, our tasks are so large that we don't even want to begin to tackle them. But as Roman philosopher Seneca once said, *"It is not because things are difficult that we do not dare; it is because we do not dare that they are difficult."* If you're suddenly tasked with creating your organization's social media presence out of nowhere, or setting up a new big branch in Shanghai, you'll feel overwhelmed, for sure. The task seems too big.

But if we work out the individual major sub-steps, and divide those major sub-steps into smaller sub-steps, the task is no longer so threatening. A valuable thought from the Chinese philosopher Lao Tzu: *"A journey of a thousand miles begins with a single step."*

Completing mammoth tasks is not only a good exercise in organizing yourself, it's also vitally important for your long-term success. You could even say, the more unpleasant the task, the more pleasant the reward when you've finished it! For example, writing an email to a colleague is easy, but writing an email with a customized offer to a potential high-paying customer who didn't sound too convinced on the phone and had a bunch of demands? Now that's hard. But it's clear which of the two emails would lead to a better deal, to more money.

So, cut the big task into such small slices that there's no more room for procrastination. No more too-big tasks—slice it up and get it done!

10 The time diary

Many manages aren't aware of how much time they spend on which task. A simple time diary in which you note down what you have done every 60 minutes or so helps you get organized quick in this respect.

Even if it seems annoying at first, the time diary very quickly fosters an awareness of what you're actually using your time for—and what you're wasting it on. When looking over your time diary, pay attention to whether you completed important tasks in your performance highs or in your performance lows. After all, a good manager knows when he's capable of peak performance during the workday—and schedules his time accordingly.

> **EXERCISE #13: Your own time diary**
>
> During the coming week, meticulously note what you did, when you did it, and for how long. After seven days, analyze your own handling of time. If it's to your liking—great! If not— now you see on paper how much amazing potential there is for improvement!

Conclusion

There you have it: the best productivity and time management techniques. You can combine many of them quite well. But you don't have to implement them all right away, of course. It would be unrealistic for you to change all of your habits overnight anyway. I bet you're already successfully using one or two of the techniques listed here. And I hope you'll try as many as possible. Give each technique a chance for at least a week or two. Using a majority, if not all of the ten techniques is incredibly helpful, especially if you consistently integrate them into your daily routine.

Leading Teams & Motivating Employees

Chapter overview:

01 Leadership styles

Of course, there are very different ways to manage your team. The main leadership styles are presented below, along with their advantages and disadvantages. And to already let the cat out of the bag: no leadership style is perfect. Rather, you should figure out which one fits you and your employees best. One thing is clear: Your leadership style can have a big impact on your employees' output and thus the entire mood of the team.

Leadership Styles

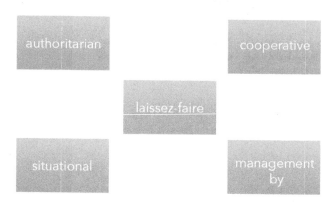

a) **Authoritarian leadership style**

With this style, the manager is at the center, giving instructions, guidelines, and holding all the strings. The authoritarian leadership style does not necessarily mean that employees' interests are not taken into account or that mistakes are harshly punished. Rather, the manager is something like an "enlightened monarch." He knows more and can do more than his employees. Yet he still lets his people advise him from time to time, and he's grateful for this good advice. Authoritarianism is therefore not to be confused with dictatorship.

The *advantages* of this leadership style are obvious: decisions are made quickly, and there are no pointless discussions and meetings. After all, employees hired by the manager also know exactly what to do and what not to do. An authoritarian leader is like a strict school teacher. He has a handle on what's going on and knows exactly what he wants and what employees should do. Chaos never breaks out. When there might be less competent employees, the authoritarian management style makes perfect sense. Rather passive and shy employees perceive strictness and clear rule-setting positively because it gives them orientation and protection.

The main *disadvantages* of the authoritarian leadership style are: First of all, its success is entirely dependent on the competence of the manager. If the manager makes a mistake in such a system, hardly anyone can raise his voice or try to correct the manager. Self-confident employees feel incapacitated, put down by such a manager. No matter how good the employee's suggestions are or what evidence he has for his own views – everything depends on the good will of the "patriarch." This can be frustrating in the long run. Secondly, such a system is also burdensome for the manager, since all responsibility rests on his shoulders. The manager becomes overburdened over time by trying to have a say in all decisions.

Especially in the 21st century, such a leadership style is usually counterproductive for intellectual jobs. Speaking quite frankly, I'd say an employee could potentially know more than any manager just with the help of Google. So, it's only reasonable for a leader to rely on the better-researched information of their own people. In an authoritarian system, on the other hand, it's difficult for employees to motivate themselves and use their own initiative to drive results forward because in the end, the boss gets all the credit anyway. However, if the authority figure is not resistant to consultation and enjoys respect among employees, the authoritarian leadership style could work well in principle (especially if employees lack certain qualifications and need the leader's competence to complete specific jobs).

b) Cooperative management style

For the cooperative management style, managers and employees meet at eye level. Discussions are explicitly welcome, and both manager and employee consider each other as partners, not as boss and subordinate.

The *advantages* of the cooperative style are, above all, increased employee motivation thanks to participation in the decision-making process, and increased independence. This model is also less intensive for the manager, since he doesn't have to oversee certain tasks at all, or only oversees them partially. In most cases, the working atmosphere here is much warmer than with the authoritarian leadership style. This also means that the willingness to perform will usually be higher.

The main *disadvantage* of the collaborative management style is strong open-discussion culture. This means that decisions usually take longer, too many meetings are scheduled, and extroverted employees dominate those meetings, wanting to put their own stamp on the teams. They virtually become self-appointed mini-managers.

In order for the cooperative management style to make sense, individual employees need to be more qualified. The cooperative style meets the expectations of most employees nowadays.

c) Laissez-faire management style

In the laissez-faire management style, employees are given the greatest possible freedom. Many Silicon Valley companies are demonstrating what is completely inconceivable in standard companies: Employees have no fixed working hours and no fixed vacation days. They can take leave when and for as long as they want. There are also no fixed weekly working hours. They decide independently what they want to work on. And in some companies, not even the salary is determined by managers, but by the team (within a defined framework and according to certain performance criteria). The supervisor in such a leadership style is only aware of general developments—and prefers not to be called "CEO" or "Manager," but simply Jeff or Sandra.

The *advantages* of this style are, above all, high job satisfaction through the greatest possible self-determination, a super relaxed working atmosphere, and almost limitless creativity (at least potentially).

The *disadvantage* is mainly the potential lack of discipline resulting in a chaotic mess. This style is also very dependent on the intrinsic motivation of the employees. That's why successful startups strive to give the company a greater sense of purpose and mission in the world, to keep employees active and engaged.

Especially in creative departments and young companies, the laissez-faire management style can be quite successful. Many million-dollar Silicon Valley start-ups have proved this.

d) Situational leadership style

With the situational leadership style, leaders adapt their interaction to the maturity level of the particular employee. *Hersey/Blanchard* thus distinguish between a total of four maturity levels:

- if the employee's **maturity level is low**, the leader should give clear instructions for easy implementation. This corresponds to the authoritarian type described above, where the boss says A and the employee does A.

- If the employee has a **low to medium maturity level**, the leader should give more direction, less instruction, but at the same time provide support. This also means justifying decisions and answering questions.

- At a **medium to high maturity level**, the employee should be actively participating, i.e. encouraged to develop his own ideas and make his own decisions.

- Finally, at a **high maturity level**, both decision-making and final implementation can be delegated to the employee.

Be aware that it's possible for one and the same employee to exhibit different maturity levels depending on the sphere of work he's involved in. So, for new tasks, make sure to give clear instructions; for regular tasks, delegate them to the employee according to his area of expertise. Ultimately, situational leadership theory is nothing more than common sense, really: Each situation and employee requires case-by-case judgment and should be managed appropriately.

The *advantage* of the situational leadership style is obvious: The manager treats each employee differently, depending on the employee's maturity level. That way, the manager facilitates a work environment more fitting to the employee than in the other three leadership styles. In the other leadership styles, one way of working is applied to all, even though it's not always well received.

The *disadvantage* of the situational leadership style is that the manager must be able to "read" the individual employee in order to find out what the employee's needs are in terms of instructions, praise, reprimands, etc. Practicing this style properly therefore requires a considerable amount of time and sophisticated job interviews (more on this in the chapter, "The Empathetic Psychologist").

e) Management by styles

The management by styles of leadership is very popular in the US. Its variations describe general leadership concepts which are simple but quite inspirational. The seven main management by variations are briefly explained below.

Management by objectives means management by agreement on objectives or results. Manager and employee jointly define goals (for a year, for example) and work together to achieve them. The great advantage of this management concept is clarity and transparency. The great disadvantage is the pressure on the employee to perform, since everything depends on the result. A decisive factor for success is the extent to which the employee is involved in defining the objectives, and the extent to which he's given the freedom to define his path to the goal (sometimes also called **management by participation**). The higher the maturity level, the higher the level of participation should be.

Management by exception means leadership is necessary only in exceptional cases, i.e., only when something goes wrong. As long as everything goes according to plan, the manager holds back, giving the employee as much room as possible. The big advantage here is that the manager is free to focus on other things while the employee takes on a high degree of responsibility. The big disadvantage is that the manager is not informed about partial steps; his intervention might therefore come too late, should any trouble arise.

Management by decision rules means that employees are given clear if-then rules to help them manage everyday tasks. This management concept is especially ideal for routine tasks.

Management by delegation means leadership through proper delegation of tasks. Tasks that an employee can do better than or just as well as the manager are delegated to said employee (more on proper delegation in the chapter "The Motivating Team Leader").

Management by motivation means that the employee is motivated to do his job with the help of extrinsic (such as salary increases or gifts) or intrinsic (such as self-fulfillment and a sense of purpose) goals (more on this in the chapter "The Motivating Team Leader").

Management by crisis means that an internal crisis is taken as an opportunity to change the corporate structures in order to prevent such a crisis from ever happening again.

Management by information means that the focus is on passing on information to employees. Employees should be informed about (almost) all areas and departments and given due opportunity to ask questions.

It's no secret that management by styles are poorly defined and heavily criticized by researchers. But their advantage is that the main characteristics of the leadership method can be summarized in just a few words, and everyone can agree on the core meaning.

Other good variations of management by styles are *management by systems*, or *management by wandering around*, among others. The overabundance of management-by styles, by the way, has led to some rather funny satire. The following is a small selection of my favorite concepts from internet forums and blogs by people with a keen sense of humor:

- **Management by decibel**: The leader convinces through high volume, not sound argumentation.

- **Management by falling fruit**: When decisions are ripe, they fall, i.e., are made by themselves.

- **Management by ping-pong**: Keep passing the work back and forth until it's passed off and out of sight.

- **Management by lemon squeezer**: The manager can always squeeze something more out of his team, if only he presses a little bit harder.

- **Management by hippo**: Being up to your neck in the mud as a manager, coming out to open your mouth every once in a while, and then going completely out of sight for a while.

- **Management by babysitter**: The manager takes care of the issues where employees are shouting the loudest.

- **Management by Herod**: After Herod the Great, an infamous Roman client king of Judea. The manager looks for a competent successor, then fires him.

- **Management by Britney Spears**: The manager's way of taking responsibility for a mistake is to just say "Oops!... I did it again!", passing off the corrective work to the employee instead.

- **Management by astronaut**: A leadership style consisting entirely of rambling and weightless remarks.

EXERCISE #14: Your current management style

Now that you know about various leadership styles, reflect briefly on your own leadership style. Are you authoritarian? Laissez faire? Above all: Do you make use of the situational leadership style? If you haven't already, make a note of potential situations where adapting your style to the individual employee's maturity level would work best.

02 Skillfully leading meetings

Meetings generally don't have a good reputation in organizations. They are time-consuming, unpleasant, and often inconclusive, which is why they are rejected by employees and managers alike. It's no wonder: In many professions, people spend about half of their working time in meetings, which last about three hours on average.

You would think that managers would naturally come to the conclusion that having so many meetings is unnecessary; many problems can also be solved via email or even a simple phone call. But often the meeting is held anyway because "planned is planned." Even when the matter is settled, a new agenda is spontaneously drafted, and those present at the meeting are either woefully unprepared or the new agenda doesn't apply to them at all. So why would they bother listening to you? According to some general studies, around one third of meeting participants conduct private business during the meeting (i.e., they're messaging on WhatsApp, Facebook, playing games, etc.). This is, unfortunately, everyday life in the working world. People get distracted if something doesn't really have anything to do with them.

Be brave and cancel the meeting when you realize you could do without it.

However, if the meeting is absolutely necessary—or you want your future meetings to 100% serve a purpose and be happily attended in the future – then you should get to know these five essential meeting types, and consider their respective benefits and challenges.

a) Informational meetings

This meeting type requires the most preparation in terms of content. But be careful: When information needs to be conveyed, we tend to pack a lot onto the slides, and the audience is quickly overwhelmed.

If you are just chairing the meeting while the employees give the presentations, have them send you the presentations ahead of time, including their duration. If you feel there is too much material, ask the staff member to shorten it, and make it clear that the scheduled speaking time must be respected. There's nothing worse than a meeting where everyone overshoots their time, and everything drags on as a result.

When chairing informational meetings, you should give a short introduction before each staff presentation. Your employees can be great experts, but without experience, it's easy to forget to put the presentation into a broader context. Such presentations simply pass the audience by, because no one is thinking it affects him. However, because you called the meeting in the first place, you and you alone know the bigger picture. It's your job to make sure everyone else is aware of the bigger picture too. So, take the time to briefly introduce the topic's larger context, and let your employees take it from there.

And don't forget about question period. You can also designate a "time guard" to give a reminder five minutes before the time is up. No matter the organization, everybody loves a bit of structure in the business world. And structure is especially important for info meetings.

Two final tips on informational meetings: First, make sure that transitions between presentations are smooth. In concrete terms, this means briefly summarizing the essence of each complete presentation in your own words while finding a thematic transition to the next presentation.

Second, be sure to give a brief general summary of the meeting at the end, emphasizing, for example, the three most important takeaways from the presentations. If you are presenting yourself, practice your speech out loud at least once. After all, you're a role model for your employees: Don't exceed the allotted time yourself, and speak smoothly and clearly. You can trust my many years of experience as a public speaker: Nothing feels better than presenting with confidence, and you can easily get that by practicing at least once at home.

b) Decision-making meetings

No trick to this one: These meetings are all about making a decision. Though, as a manager, you can provide clear direction and thus significantly influence the decision. But even if you have a crystal-clear direction: Don't show all your cards at once. Have employees debate, discuss, refute, collect examples, and analyze empirical data (including from competitors) about pros and cons (for example).

Your role here is to ensure that all decision-related options are put on the table and backed up with arguments.

The greatest danger in decision-making meetings is *groupthink*. The phenomenon, which was first studied at length by Irving Janis around 1972, describes the tendency of group members to consciously or unconsciously adjust their opinions to the expected group opinion. The employee wants to have not just any opinion, but the "right" one; he's afraid of stepping out of line. This leads to a situation where not every possible course of action is duly analyzed. Instead, most employees tend to gravitate to one solution right away, and this tendency intensifies over time.

The *Asch conformity experiments* from the 1950s showed that people will go along with the majority opinion even when they know that the majority opinion is objectively wrong. All of that just to avoid getting kicked out of the group.

So, what can you do about groupthink? First off, strongly opinionated participants in the group should be curbed from completely dominating the conversation. However, and second, the leader should make it clear that different opinions are still very welcome. And third, arguments should be presented on all courses of action.

My favorite way to conduct a decision meeting is through debate. In the debate process, positions are assigned to employees and each is given five minutes to speak for his side. Whether the employee herself also represents his assigned position is irrelevant. It's about getting as many pro and con arguments on the table as possible. To make sure it flows smoothly: First, someone from the pro side speaks, then someone from the con side, then someone from the pro side again, and so on and so forth.

A decision debate like this can be really fun and is one of the most popular exercises I use as a coach for leadership training. You, as a leader, could also interpose various questions to spice things up a bit. You can also consider participating in the debate yourself. If not, you can be a "judge," taking notes of the best arguments and then going over them with employees. This kind of a debate makes groupthink near impossible.

As an alternative to a debate, you could also organize for a session of anonymous feedback sharing. You would read the anonymous statements aloud and then discuss them with the present team.

But in the end, the decision meeting is about making a decision. It's best to communicate the decision-making procedure to employees in advance to ensure absolute transparency.

One last tip: If you're moderating the decision meeting, make sure that all irrelevant issues are excluded. This type of meeting is all about making a specific decision to take action.

c) Brainstorming meetings

Brainstorming is not just for creative departments; all departments of an organization could use good ideas. The question is: How do you organize a brainstorm meeting so that as many employees as possible participate in it to get a great result?

First of all, the main (leading) question for the meeting is important. The question shouldn't be general or all-encompassing ("What can we do better in our company?"). Brainstorming also has two phases for which clear rules apply:

Phase 1 is about generating as many ideas as possible, so criticism and praise are prohibited here. Any other form of irrelevant comment should also be omitted. If participants violate these rules, you should discreetly draw their attention to the rules again. The crazier or more creative the idea sounds, the better. Furthermore, participants can be inspired by other ideas during the meeting, which they can combine with their own idea to help generate something original. Task one of your employees with writing down the ideas during this phase. The phase should last no more than 20-30 minutes. It could even be shorter. It's meant to be a quick burst of ideas, not a marathon.

The ideas are then collected in **phase 2**, sorted into clusters, and evaluated one by one. This may well take longer, and experts can also be consulted if it is not clear whether an idea is actually feasible.

Brainstorming is the most popular creativity technique in the world. But it has its fair share of skeptics. I can still remember an article in the online *ZEIT Campus* with the title, "Brainstorming is Bullshit." An experiment done by Utrecht University was cited in which groups generated 20 to 50% fewer ideas than people working individually. In the study, the group's ideas were also deemed less creative. Researchers suggested that the group's failure was due to loud shouting, which disturbed people's ability to think clearly. Other ideas also distracted participants from their own inner thought processes. And the system seemed to favor spontaneous people, because some people simply needed more time to come up with ideas. There were problems with hierarchies too, of course; the shy and timid didn't want to embarrass themselves in front of the boss.

Under these unfavorable circumstances, it's not really surprising that individuals come up with more and better ideas than groups of individuals. But does that truly make brainstorming bullshit? Not at all! As a moderator, the manager can create a good atmosphere, make people forget about office hierarchies, and let everyone know that no matter how silly or odd sounding, every idea is welcome. You can even look at the apparent downsides positively: Ideas from others can interrupt my thought process, or, they can really kick-start it. Sometimes, your own idea only really gets going when another coworker provides the inspiration for it. It's all about having the right circumstances and appropriate environment for brainstorming.

You should also let employees think on their own at the beginning. Discuss all the ideas together afterwards. That way, the advantages of individual work (full concentration) and the advantages of the group phase (mutual inspiration) can be combined for a great result. Or, you can design phase 1 completely anonymously and collect ideas only in writing. You could use an electronic meeting system for that purpose, also called **brainwriting**. The advantage of anonymity is that no one knows which idea comes from the boss and which from the coworker. Again, phase 1 should take place without judgment and evaluations. Only in phase 2 are ideas discussed and analyzed.

Whether brainstorming or brainwriting, it's best to try both and see which method your team finds better for generating creative ideas (and which one is more fun!). By the way, the most innovative ideas often don't come from experts at all, but from colleagues who are only indirectly involved, or even not involved at all. This is because experts often think in terms of system constraints and rarely think outside the box. So, invite colleagues who are not directly involved to the brainstorming or brainwriting session in the interest of plentiful ideas. In phase 2, you can then discuss (only) with your experts which "crazy" idea just might be feasible after all.

d) Training meetings

The fourth meeting type is for training and education. There are generally two options here: either hire an external consultant, or organize the training yourself.

If you bring in an external consultant, you should not only pay attention to their expertise and recommendations, but also make sure that the training is tailored to the team's needs. For me, personally, when I'm booked by a company for leadership training, or negotiation or rhetoric seminars, it's usually through the HR department. The boss doesn't take the time to talk to me as a trainer. Instead, he lets the recruiter decide and usually either only gives one budget, or says he's still looking at three other offers. He then decides without having talked to me, the coach. Only about one in seven managers actually takes the time to explain to me for 20–30 minutes exactly what his team needs.

In my experience, the HR manager often doesn't know what exactly the specialist team needs. The manager knows best, so he needs to participate! Another problem: The external trainer can hardly say to the personnel manager, "P*ut your boss on the phone, please; he needs to discuss the focus of the training with me."* This could easily seem too intrusive, and the trainer doesn't want to jeopardize his assignment, but he also needs to be able to deliver the best possible result. On the other hand, the average trainer is just happy to have sold a seminar. He'd have no problem dishing out his tried-and-true methods with as little comment from upper management as possible – like a high school teacher who has been using the same book templates for 20 years.

But some managers are doing it just right: You make a telephone appointment with me as a trainer for at least 30 minutes, tell me in detail about your company values, any communication difficulties, and desired content and exercises. Your involvement increases the practical relevance and quality of the training enormously. The employees are also much happier because the trainer isn't just talking their ears off. Instead, they have targeted conversations about the specific communication challenges in *their* organization.

So, when you book an outside trainer, take that half hour to show your chosen trainer what you and your team really need.

If you conduct the training internally, i.e., by yourself or an employee, make sure that the info is easily digestible and poignant. In other words, no one should need a PhD to understand the session. The internal trainer should

   I.   start simple, and only slowly go into more depth;
  II. explain well and prepare nice, neat examples; and
 III. always be open to sudden questions.

That's it. More than that is unnecessary. One last idea for the training meeting in general: If you frequently conduct internal training, an outside perspective can be quite enlightening. For example, I was recently asked to provide rhetorical training to executives at the Munich Police Headquarters. They previously only had internal police training. These trainings had very specific internal criteria, which were good, but somewhat one-sided. It was very important for the police executives to get completely different feedback via an external party—feedback on how others viewed them as a police force, for example. That way, they were able to try out completely new exercises. From time to time, influences from the outside can do wonders for your team.

e) AMA Meetings

The last meeting type is very popular in modern US companies: the *Ask-Me-Anything meeting*. Here, the manager answers any and all questions from the team. The questions can either be collected anonymously or asked directly during the meeting. If there's an existing open communication culture, the latter is preferable; if there is a suboptimal communication culture, anonymous is preferred. Otherwise, no one will speak up.

An AMA meeting comes with numerous benefits. First, the questions are **honest feedback**. Managers immediately recognize what people are unhappy with and know how employees think. Managers really shouldn't fear critical feedback as much as they do. With any critical feedback, there are only two options: Either the criticism is not justified, in which case you should of course explain why that is the case; or, the criticism is justified, in which case you can take it up as an idea and make processes or products better from there. Honest feedback allows the company to learn faster and improve in the long run.

If you're worried that you won't come up with a good or quick-witted answer on the spot, why not just collect the questions a day or two in advance and think about the answers before presenting them?

Second, with an AMA meeting, you can **clear up misconceptions**. It's no secret that rumors and talk float around in many departments. An AMA meeting is a great way to make a clear stand and put an end to any rumors. Employee misconceptions, which are not even consciously directed against the company, can be detected and corrected, too.

And third, **employees feel heard** because the manager gives them the opportunity to interact directly. Many companies worldwide are miles away from an open feedback culture. In many countries, authoritarian thinking and hierarchies play a decisive role in many industries. So, hardly any employee dares to go to the boss and openly criticize him. However, this also means that the employee does not feel heard in the status quo; he feels unfairly treated in the long run. But even there, anonymous feedback could allow him to vent his frustration (which is good in itself), giving him a direct line to the boss.

All in all, AMA meetings are wonderful for cultivating relationships with the team. I definitely recommend them.

f) Ten general rules for meetings

There are a few good general rules for meetings that you can use as a checklist before each meeting. Follow the rules, and give your employees the best possible meeting experience.

10 General Rules for Meetings

1. Always start and end the meeting on time.

2. Send all participants a detailed agenda and handouts at least a day before.

3. Only who needs to be there should be there.

4. Select a chairman (even yourself) to keep track of time, monitor topic relevance, and politely intervene when needed.

5. Send out the summary/minutes/call-to-action to each participant after the meeting, preferably the same day.

6. Keep it to one or two topics.

7. Never have "Other Matters" as a topic; it's a timewaster.

8. Stand during the meeting. It ends quicker that way, and the participants are at your full attention, not slouching in their seats.

9. No snacks; they're just distracting.

10. Where possible, ask all participants to do without electronics for the meeting (phones, laptops, tablets).

EXERCISE #15: Your own meetings

Now, please analyze your own meetings. Critically examine whether and how you can integrate those ten meeting rules into your everyday work life.

03 Be a team leader, be a group leader

It's very useful to learn about meeting types and their specific challenges. But that's only half the story. In the end, groups are made up of individuals, each with his own talents and needs. They exist in every meeting: classic representations of certain personality types.

Let's start with this beautiful zoo meeting here and analyze all the characters, one by one, in a clockwise direction starting from the bottom left corner. Our first protagonist is the **biting dog, the fighter**. He is intent on stirring up conflict within the team. He loves confrontation and feels brave enough to take the manager on too. Now, you can't re-educate him – or any other character, for that matter. So, how do you best "lead" the fighter? The answer: Stay calm and do not respond to the provocations, because they would be counterproductive for the group.

People often ask me here: "How am I supposed to stay calm when the other person is being an asshole and just looking for a fight?" Fair enough. Staying calm on the inside requires emotional training, which doesn't interest everyone, it's a lengthy process, and it contains enough material for an entire book. But there's also a quick remedy: If you feel provoked by the arguer, just don't show it on the outside. Pay attention while maintaining a calm voice and slow body language. No one can tell that you're almost bursting with anger on the inside. If you pretend to be calm on the outside, that's often enough.

Then, present the other person's provocative ideas for discussion in the group. This action alone can also discreetly lead the group to doubt and refute the ideas of the arguer. For example, try saying: *"Interesting idea. I feel like the idea is worth discussing. What do the others think?"* That way, you cleverly avoid direct confrontation and, through your (outwardly) calm manner, send the other person a clear message that there will be no dispute.

Let's continue through our zoo meeting. The **horse** is **the positive** in the group. You should include him in the discussion, especially if it becomes negative. The positive is also wonderful for good summaries. Don't use him too often—instead, save that energy for lightening the mood during tense times.

The next ideal type of meeting participant is **the know-it-all**, represented here in the form of a **monkey**. He's the eager beaver in school: well-prepared, answers questions immediately, and usually gives good answers. With the know-it-all, make sure he doesn't get to speak too often. As many people as possible need to be able to participate in the meeting. But give him the tough questions, for sure; the monkey is the best candidate to answer them. He's the know-it-all, after all: your jack-of-all-trades for tough questions. You could also use performance incentives to motivate the know-it-all, be they development, status, or monetary incentives. They'll eat it up, because they want something. Find out what the know-it-all really wants to work on, and let him have a go at it. You can read more about how to find out what an employee really wants in the next chapter, "The Empathetic Psychologist."

If the know-it-all interrupts the others inconsiderately or comments rudely (by explaining why a coworker's answer was stupid, for example), then make him pump the brakes. In a performance review, you can definitely praise his smart qualities, but make it clear to him that he should not be a lone wolf his entire career; he needs to be a team player. Skillfully incentivize and reward him for his teamwork, making him realize its obvious benefits.

So, let's move on to the frog, who croaks a lot but doesn't say much. You guessed it: The **frog** is **the talkative one**. With him, the "mirror technique" helps. Simply point out that he talks much more than his colleagues, and that he should please be more brief. Like this: "Mr. Muller, have you noticed that your speeches are longer and more frequent than those of your colleagues?" You have to be persistent with him. That is, when he rambles on again, keep pointing this out to him. Two or three times is not enough. The talkative person probably got the bad habit because no one took the time to correct him, remind him that he talks too much. Using the mirror technique, you make it clear to him that he won't get far with rambling on from now on.

The **antelope** represents **the shy one**. Low self-esteem makes him afraid to participate. It's therefore your job, as team leader, to engage him in the discussion with easy questions and discreetly praise his answers. This might encourage him to enter the discussion on his own, too.

The **hedgehog** is **the rejector**. He puts his spikes up at new proposals and knows 100 reasons why something won't work. He's often not at all wrong and can refer to experience if necessary. Naturally, he always sees things rather negatively. However, listen more closely to his reasons for rejecting things. Most of the time, they're good reasons for you not to implement a proposal; or they're good reasons for changing something. At the very least, he will cause you to be more careful. That can be an advantage!

The **hippo** is **the not-interested one**. He fades into the background in every meeting session, and says absolutely nothing. He also frequently makes this absent facial expression, indicating his mind's somewhere else. How can you bring him back to the surface? If nothing about your meeting interests him, he is—like most people—self-centered and likes to talk about himself and his own projects. Simply ask him about his current activities and plans. He will be happy to show up mentally, then.

The **giraffe** is **the big honcho**, that is, an important or *the* most important person in the room. The big honcho is also referred to as the HIPPO, too, actually ("**h**ighest **p**aid **p**erson's **o**pinion"). But back to the giraffe as the big honcho: This could be your own superior who is present at the meeting. So, what to do with the big beast? The most important thing is to not criticize him, neither directly nor indirectly. He will notice if you do. Of course, you shouldn't be buttering him up either. Carefully put his views into perspective instead, using phrases like, *"On the one hand, yes, on the other hand ...,"* or, *"You are absolutely right on that point, and you could also add ...,"* or, *"At this point I would like to add that ..."* The last two formulations in particular have no element of tension. They're ideal to use on superiors who cannot tolerate even the slightest contradiction.

By the way, the big honcho can also be a universally respected colleague who is below you in the office hierarchy but nonetheless enjoys the greatest popularity among employees. He often has this status not only because of his high level of expertise, but also because he is intensively committed to the interests of the team. Make him your friend, your ally, and pay special tribute to his contributions.

Our last animal is **the questioner**, represented here as the cunning **fox**. He asks in detail, notes everything down, and draws attention to things you failed to make clear or explain properly. Open some of his questions to the group, and answer some of them yourself. The fox comes across to many as an annoying colleague. But you know that his questions serve a purpose: They point out gaps that you and the team can fill. He is a kind of logical perfectionist who wants to know everything. His questions will ultimately bring you and your team to answer more thoroughly. However, you should stop his questioning when it comes to topics that are unimportant for the team. Because with the fox, the Pareto principle applies, according to which you can be satisfied with just 80% if something is not entirely relevant.

These nine personality types in meetings are not the only ones, but they're the most common. Some rare ones might still crop up. If the **class clown** is there, you need to have a one-on-one conversation with him right away to set some boundaries. The important thing with him is not to ban jokes completely, but to find the right balance between entertainment and distraction for the team. Then there is the **snake**, i.e., an employee who mostly plots intrigues, but also occasionally bullies other employees. You should take action against the snake with all the force of labor law, should it come to that. Bullying is not fun for anyone. The **black sheep** might also be there. You, as a manager, should show him in a one-on-one meeting how to adhere to the norms of the group and slowly be accepted by it again.

Other characters that can also be found in offices: the **smombie (smartphone zombie)**, the **diva**, the **snacker**, the **latecomer**, and many others. In general, with these characters, you should not only ask yourself how best to explain to them that they should abide by group rules. As a good leader, you also need to look for reasons why a person behaves in a certain way, because sometimes it's possible to permanently remove the unpleasant behavior from meetings through psychological root cause analysis (more on this in the chapter "The Empathetic Psychologist").

EXERCISE #16: Employees and personality types

Make a list of all your employees. Assign each employee one of the roles shown above. Then, think about how you should react and act with the particular employee to best develop his potential in the group. Don't forget to implement these tips for your next meeting!

04 Correct delegation

The biggest advantage for the manager who can properly delegate tasks is that he gains more time for doing important tasks. Still, many managers find it hard to let go a bit. The loss of control, coupled with the fear that something won't be done right, leads managers to prefer to do everything themselves.

A great quote often attributed to Theodore Roosevelt:

> "The best executive is the one who has sense enough to pick good men to do what he wants done, and self-restraint to keep from meddling with them while they do it."

But how to pick the right people for the right job? Let's look at the three levels of delegating.

The three levels of delegating

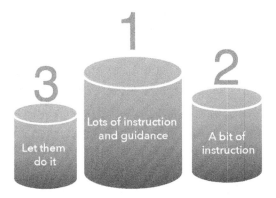

At **level 1**, you're dealing with an employee who has a *low maturity level*. Here, in the interest of both parties, it is important that the manager gives as precise instructions as possible (preferably step by step). This increases the probability that the task will be done right, and the manager doesn't have to worry about it. It's also good for the employee because he has little experience himself, so he's grateful for a detailed briefing on the task. The employee doesn't want to screw anything up, either. It's best for the manager to create precise guidelines here. That way, he gives the employee the confidence to complete the task.

At **level 2**, you have an employee with a *medium maturity level* on your hands. Here, you still make the final decision on the task (as a manager), but you also let the employee do the preliminary work (e.g. research, outlining, drafting, etc.). This can look something like this: the employee independently familiarizes himself with a new topic, and then he reports to you on the most important points or options. You then decide which of the options is best for your organization. If you ask your employee to do more, have him weigh the options and make a recommendation about what he thinks would be the best option for the organization. Here, of course, the employee should address the alternatives as well, and collect pros and cons for the main options. That way, you get the full picture and can decide from there.

Level 3 is about delegating not only the implementation, but the entire decision to the employee. This third form of delegating is suitable for employees with a *high maturity level*. Two things can happen here: Either you ask the employee to tell you a bit about his final decision, or you trust him to the point that you don't need feedback on how things went with the task.

Level 3 involves a lot of employee responsibility, but even new managers shouldn't be afraid to try it out. If you know your employees well and know exactly what their strengths are already, then why not? With these three levels, you can give each employee tasks that match his ability to get the job done. Delegating appropriately is also in line with the situational management style.

It all sounds so simple and reasonable, but many managers still have problems with making consistent and appropriate use of the three levels of delegating. Now, why is that?

a) Inner objections to delegating

Managers don't delegate enough and thereby waste valuable time because of certain inner dogmas. These dogmas ultimately prevent him from trusting others to do the work too. Let's take a closer look at the five most common inner dogmas.

b) "It takes too long to explain—I'd rather do it myself!"

First of all, it should be noted that level 1 delegating is the only level that requires detailed and time-consuming explanation. Second, you could actually delegate the explaining to an experienced employee, who could tell the less experienced employee what to do, step by step.

But even if there is no such experienced employee: Think of level 1 delegating as an important, one-time investment. Sure, you lose a few hours of time writing down all the instructions and talking them through. But you save time in the future, since the employee will be able to do these kinds of tasks without needing new instruction.

Also, the great thing about a standard task guide is that it can be used by other employees. For example, if the rookie leaves after her probationary period and you hire someone else, you can refer back to the guide. So (and this is another good tip in general), always put standardized processes and explanations in writing. It saves you a huge amount of time in the long run.

c) "I can do it better—the employee is not as competent as I am!"

You may be able to do the job better than any employee or colleague on your team. But the question is: Does this particular task need to be 100% perfectly executed? Even with important tasks, sometimes 80% perfection is enough. And surely there is someone on the team who can achieve that 80% just as well as you! Maybe even just 50% is enough for a certain task. If that's the case, all the more reason to let someone else take care of it!

Taking on a task yourself only makes sense if it's of the highest priority. Such a task is important and urgent, has far-reaching financial or corporate consequences, and it requires your specific skill set.

d) "I'll do it faster myself!"

It may be that you can handle the matter faster than your employees. What takes you one hour might take an employee four. Is it thus more efficient to do it yourself?

The answer is: no. Your time—the manager's time—is simply more valuable than that of your employees. You can talk all you want about flat hierarchies and calling your boss "Bob" instead of "Mr. Roberts," but not all employees have the same responsibilities, experience, and foresight as the manager. After all, you weren't promoted to manager for nothing. It's not your job to *micromanage* (meddle everywhere), but to make strategic decisions. Once you have tasks that need completing, delegate them to free up time for the bigger picture—even if it's just to free up an hour to think about process and structural optimization, for example. Seriously, take the time. *Macro management* is your main responsibility, not micro.

e) "I'll lose control if I don't do it myself!"

Letting go of or losing control is not necessarily part of delegating. Only the third level of delegating encourages you to transfer the authority to implement and make decisions to an employee. After all, at levels 1 and 2, ultimate decision-making remains with you.

So if you feel that you don't want to relinquish control on a particular task for some reason, then simply retain final say on completing that task. However, you should be sure to relinquish authority to make decisions at least part of the time.

By allowing employees more and more freedom, especially those with a high level of maturity, the employees' skills and abilities grow with the ever-increasing tasks. This increases employee motivation because most people enjoy working independently and making their own decisions (more on motivation in the sub-chapter, "Motivating employees").

f) "If I delegate, it makes it look like I can't do it myself!"

First of all, no one will expect you to be able to do everything yourself. It even makes a leader more likable to admit her own weaknesses and trust the strengths of her employees. Secondly, your team is there to support you with tasks and take on the things that the team can manage itself.

If you're smart, you will not only admit where you could use a hand, but you will have the employee explain in detail (if it's relevant) how he can help you solve that task. I know from my experience as a business coach that most managers are extremely reluctant to do this. They see it as a sign of weakness. But here, too, it helps to remember that when an employee can do something better than you, you gain time for even more important tasks. Your own pride should not stand in the way of working efficiently.

g) "I don't want to impose anything on my colleagues I can do myself!"

In order to be popular and liked by everyone, a new manager often takes on tasks that could just as easily be done by an employee.

But in doing that, he loses focus on macro management; he gets lost in the "nitty gritty" of everyday business. He becomes just like his employees—a promoted employee getting work done, sure, but not the work of a leader. And in the long run, however, the manager's own supervisor will notice that he's making few strategic decisions. He's not giving his supervisor any reason to consider promoting him to higher leadership roles.

Don't be like that manager. Take on the role of leader with confidence: the confidence in knowing that it's your job to assign tasks, not win a popularity contest. It's your job to realize the bigger picture and steer your organization in the right direction. If you remain transparent and delegate tasks in a fair and understandable way, no employee will hold this against you, especially when you ask them for help and to be part of the process.

h) The limits of delegating

But there are, of course, tasks which should not or may not be delegated. Determining which tasks to delegate and which not ultimately depends on the organization and how it's structured. That said, here are a few ideas about what tasks you generally shouldn't delegate.

First, tasks that involve a great deal of risk or consequence should not be delegated. These and all their consequences should be handled by the manager himself.

Second, classic managerial tasks, such as conducting employee interviews or recruiting, should not be delegated. This is a matter of principle.

Other than that, delegating should become part of your daily work and give you the space you need to make strategic decisions.

Finally, let's take a look at the literature. In reading up on correct delegation, one often reads that C-tasks are to be delegated according to the Eisenhower principle—so, tasks which are not important but urgent can be delegated. This looks quite plausible at first glance. But I absolutely cannot recommend using the Eisenhower principle in this way. Why?

Again, the issue here is one of productivity. Being productive means working in a focused, effective, and efficient manner towards the goal you have set for yourself. However, as you have seen, only important tasks help you get closer to your goal. Urgent tasks (C-tasks), by definition, have nothing to do with the target. In other words: An effective manager should encourage employees to devote only a bit of time to urgent tasks, because the real focus is on the *important* B tasks.

Email is a great example of this. In many professions, there's a flood of emails. Employees regularly receive up to 100 emails a day or more. They are thus busy most of the day working through these emails. What's even worse: They also get an immediate response from some people, so the mountain of emails doesn't get any less—it only gets bigger. Most of the time, these emails are also formulated in such a way that they sound very urgent when, in reality, they might not actually be all that urgent.

Of course there are jobs, such as support jobs, where answering emails is the bread and butter of the work. But most office jobs have, or should have, a different focus. And so employees in many offices simply become automated answering machines. They rarely get the chance to do their actual work.

Clear rules on your part can help against your employees becoming email robots. Make it clear which tasks are important, i.e., which tasks they should be spending most of the day on. Feel free to delegate B tasks to employees as well. If you work on B tasks all by yourself—as most of the literature suggests that managers do—you simply won't get as far as you could with the help of your team. Use the three levels of delegating to determine who should get what task, and follow through with it. You can also delegate A-tasks with a clear conscience if you have something even more important and urgent to do at the moment. Get into the habit of letting your employees focus on doing only those things that help your organization achieve its goals—this will increase your overall productivity. This works best (as described in the first chapter of the book, "The Convincing Communicator") when you define values and goals precisely and communicate them clearly. After all, it's also the manager's job to delegate only meaningful activities and give employees immediate feedback when they're spending too much time on unimportant tasks.

EXERCISE #17: Your to-delegate list

Write down all the tasks you need to do at the moment. Assign individual tasks to the appropriate employees while taking into account their respective maturity levels. Think about how you will explain your specific task to the person, including what implementation and decision-making authority you will give them. Only a few tasks should remain on your list which cannot be delegated.

05 Conducting successful negotiations

As a manager, you're able to conduct negotiations independently, whether they're for customers (keyword: sales negotiations) or employees (keyword: salary negotiations). An intuitive knowledge of negotiation is something many people have, actually. However, sound theoretical knowledge can help you master any negotiation situation, no matter how complex.

In the following you will get a short introduction to the world's most recognized negotiation model: the *Harvard concept*. The Harvard concept (a.k.a. principled negotiation) goes back to the American legal scholars Roger Fisher and William Ury and their research into successful negotiation. Its goal is the famous "win-win solution." Here are the four fundamental Harvard principles.

a) Harvard principle #1: Separate the people from the problem.

Negotiations should always be fact-based and solution-oriented. Especially in conflict situations, personal attacks and unpleasant remarks by negotiating partners must be completely eliminated. Therefore, the maxim is to always focus on the facts and—even if you are attacked or treated rudely—never stoop to the personal level. Even if an agreement is not reached after strenuous negotiations, you should not express your feelings either way. It is quite possible that you will encounter the same party again later, and personal grudges from bad experiences would only hinder future business.

The exciting question is, of course: How do you refrain from outwardly showing negative feelings in conflict situations? The quick answer is to simply take a break from negotiating, review the situation, and analyze exactly why the other person was so quick-tempered or frustrating. Everyone knows that negative feelings or strong emotions subside over time. So, the more time passes, the less we feel disappointed, annoyed, or frightened.

You can take a break from negotiating by suggesting a coffee break, for example. Or you might need to take an urgent phone call. Perhaps it's already lunch time. The main thing is to get out of the negatively charged situation because—and this is the reasoning behind the first principle—your negative emotions cloud your judgment of facts. And poor judgment makes reaching a deal less likely. The negotiation professional will therefore never mix the personal with the factual.

b) Principle #2: Focus on interests, not positions.

First, you need to know the difference between position and interest. Position is *what* a party demands. Interest in the sense of the Harvard concept means *why* a party holds this position. Interest is the motivation and logic behind a certain negotiating position. While clear negotiating positions signal strength, they can also be very inflexible and even prevent solutions that take into account mutual interest.

It therefore makes more sense for both negotiating parties to disclose their underlying interests rather than persist with strong, immovable positions. Disclosing interests makes it easier to find compromises. Only those who know the interests of the other can also make suggestions that bring the other on board, you see.

According to the Harvard concept, negotiating partners should talk explicitly and honestly about their mutual interests. That way, they find the largest *zone of possible agreement*, i.e., the greatest possible overlap of interests. It's how ideal negotiation results and win-win situations become possible. But if the parties stubbornly stick to their original positions, there's only a very small chance of finding the greatest possible overlap of interests (because you don't even know what the other person's interests are).

How can you find out the (usually unspoken) interest of the other person? With smart questions! Questions are the most important tool in a negotiation. With the correct use of various questioning techniques, experienced negotiators succeed in involving the customer in the conversation. They obtain important information and bring the sometimes deliberately hidden interests to light. Questions can have various consequences, however, so it's essential that the negotiators know which question is best for which situation. Here is a brief overview of the essential forms of questions in negotiation situations:

Open questions (Who? How? What? Where? Why?). These are ideal for learning about motives, facts, and background information.

Closed questions (answered with "yes" or "no"). They're ideal if you want to get a definitive answer. Closed questions are great for confirming an agreement or obtaining the other person's final commitment.

Alternative questions (A or B?). In the case of alternative questions, the negotiating partner is given a choice between several options. Choices can be deliberately narrowed to steer the other party in a particular direction.

Counter questions: ("And what do you say to that?"). These are especially useful if you don't have an answer to an important question from your negotiating partner right away. A counter-question can give you the time you need to think things over, providing you a clue as to the kind of answer the other person is expecting from you.

Solution-oriented questions ("What would the deal have to look like for you to agree to it?"). This question is my absolute favorite in negotiations. You get straight to the point: You want to know what conditions must be met in order for the other person to say "yes." This question speeds up the agreement immensely because it lets you know immediately what matters most to the other person.

The authors of the Harvard concept emphasize that good questions separate the wheat from the chaff. While novice negotiators ask few or no questions, it's not uncommon for negotiation professionals to ask eight to ten questions during a negotiation situation. Those who ask, know more. And as we all know, knowledge is power.

c) Principle #3: Invent options for mutual gain.

In tough negotiations, different options for a solution must be sought and evaluated. The Harvard concept provides for a strict separation between idea generation and idea evaluation (similar to brainstorming). You should therefore find as many options or proposed solutions as possible before criticizing them. This avoids rashly ruling out alternatives which might offer a suitable solution for both parties.

Again, beginners usually only bring one option for a solution to the table, whereas professionals bring a bunch of options. And if this one option is rejected by the negotiating partner, then the potential deal is already off. Negotiation professionals, on the other hand, develop four to five alternatives in advance of the conversation. This naturally makes agreement more likely. As you can see, good preparation is key. Quite a few negotiation theorists even say that the phase *before* the negotiation (i.e., preparation) is the most important. Not only can you work out options for a solution ahead of time, but you can also empathize with the other person's position and consider in advance what the other party's interests and alternatives might be.

d) Principle #4: Insist on objective criteria.

If the positions of both parties won't budge, objective evaluation criteria can help to reach an agreement. Simple if-then scenarios or objective benchmarks such as market prices or technical standards can help here. However, objective criteria must be provable: If reference is made to an "average market price," providing corresponding price statistics should be possible. The beauty of objective criteria is that they cannot be doubted; they provide both parties with security and common ground.

I'd recommend you memorize these four Harvard principles and apply them in every negotiation. A good example is a salary negotiation. When an employee comes to you with a request for a raise, "more money" is his initial position. You should now find out why he wants more money, what's the underlying interest. Perhaps he is more concerned with recognition rather than financial gain. And that could be accomplished through a bigger office or a more important job title or by giving him more responsibility—not necessarily with a monetary raise.

Always remember this when negotiating: *"You don't get what you deserve in life; you get what you negotiate."* This along with the four principles presented above will help you negotiate more for yourself.

And one last note: Negotiations are not just the formal negotiation situations. Negotiations take place dozens of times a day without you noticing. Think of it this way: Every suggestion or proposal another person makes to you—and every one you make—initiates a (small) negotiation situation. If, for example, an employee proposes to leave two hours earlier today in exchange for staying two hours longer tomorrow, this is nothing other than a negotiation situation. Or if an assistant suggests that from now on a certain task should be done directly by the employee and no longer by her because it's more efficient that way—this is also the beginning of a negotiation. Negotiations occur on a daily basis, which is why mastering the negotiation situation is an integral part of mastering the art of leadership.

EXERCISE #17: Be aware of daily negotiation potential

For one week, write down proposals that your employees, customers, and your own supervisor make to you. You'll probably notice how you could have negotiated better in these situations. And for each of the suggestions or proposals you received, think about what your ideal negotiation situation would have looked like.

06 Motivating employees

How can you best motivate employees? Research into motivation has been trying to answer this crucial question for decades. It's *the* million-dollar question because if people knew the answer, they'd be making millions with their highly motivated employees. It's the truth: most people go to work mainly to earn money— without much motivation.

Some research claims that it is impossible to motivate another person from the outside. But it's not all that bleak. There definitely are tools we can use to set the right incentives for favorably shaping employee behavior and attitudes towards company goals. A basic distinction can be made here between transactional and transformational leadership. Let's take a closer look at this and some motivational tools.

a) Transactional leadership

In this type of management, the transaction, i.e. the exchange, takes center stage. A classic example is an annual target agreement, where you look at the end of the year to see whether the employee has achieved or even exceeded the target. You reward him (exchange an advantage) for his work with a bonus, promotion, salary increase, or something similar. If the employee has not achieved the goal, you might have to give him a salary reduction (exchange a disadvantage), withhold a salary increase, reduce monetary benefits via the company, or something of the sort.

The focus here is on factual exchange: The employee gives something, and depending on what and how much it is, the manager gives back an appropriate return. The term **extrinsic motivation** has also come into use for this form of leadership. The motivation for the employee therefore consists of an incentive set from the outside, not from within himself.

External incentives work very well, at least in the short term. A famous experiment on this comes from Dan Ariely, probably the most popular motivational researcher today. At a computer chip manufacturing plant, employees were motivated in three different ways at the beginning of the week:

- *The first part of the workforce would get a salary bonus for good work—about $30 more a day.*

- *The second part of the workforce was promised praise for good work, from the boss himself.*

- *The third group was promised pizza vouchers.*

The result?

Compared to the control group, the salary bonus group produced 4.9% more computer chips after the first day. However, over the course of the week, the productivity of the bonus group dropped by 6.5% and was thus below the performance of the control group, which was not promised anything.

The praise group came in second place with a 6.6% increase in productivity. The praise group also remained above the control group at the end of the week. The winner was actually the pizza group. It had a 6.7% increase in productivity and was more productive than the control group at the end of the week.

As you can see from this experiment, extrinsic motivation may work quite well. The results are not outrageous, of course, and they subside after a while in all three variants—in this case, after just a few days. Interesting about the experiment, though, is that money performed the worst. So, meaningful praise is both cheaper and more effective.

Note that all three groups were "transactionally" managed. Pizza wasn't just given. It was given in exchange for above-average performance.

But here the fundamental problem of transactional leadership becomes apparent: People are motivated only briefly, perform better only for a short time. Soon, they get used to the new standard and fall back to their original performance level.

This is an unsatisfactory result for any manager, of course. Good thing there's also transformational leadership.

Transformational leadership

In this type of leadership, the focus is not on the transaction, but on changing attitudes and feelings. Simply put, the employee—regardless of performance—should feel good. He should be certain he's doing a meaningful task. He should know that he's collaborating on a larger vision that brings something good not only to the organization itself, but to society as whole.

If the employee maintains these positive feelings and attitudes himself and wants to work towards these goals of his own free will, then he has intrinsic motivation, the motivation from within. But how can a manager instill these attitudes and beliefs in the employee, and therefore unlock the employee's potential for internal motivation?

A leader becomes a transformational leader through four behaviors (according to Bernard Brass):

- **Idealized influence** This is about the *manager* acting *as a role model* for his employees, both professionally and personally. The manager himself is motivated, positive, takes time for the employees' concerns, and also moves the company forward with good ideas. This leadership behavior could also be called "charismatic leadership," as German sociologist Max Weber might say.

- **Inspirational motivation** Here, intrinsic motivation is established by the manager painting an *attractive vision* that employees are eager to help achieve. The activity conveys meaning and is thus an independent value for the employee. For example, let's imagine a rhetoric academy. The purpose or vision of the academy could be to free people from stage fright and speechlessness, and turn them into self-confident and eloquent people. In this way, the somewhat theoretical job of rhetoric trainer is combined with a meaningful activity that serves the people.

- **Intellectual stimulation** People naturally want to face challenges. *Intellectual challenges* in particular play a role in this, as almost everyone wants to prove themselves and their brain power. Who doesn't feel good when they come up with a good idea that works? The particular challenge for the manager here is to provide an appropriate intellectual challenge for the employee. Most people still remember the deep disappointment about not being able to solve an intellectual problem in school, way back when. It can keep them from wanting to take on similar intellectual challenges. And that's another big difficulty. You need to know exactly the maturity level of an employee in order to stimulate them intellectually.

- **Individualized Consideration** Similar to the third point, this is about an *individualized approach* to the employee. The manager becomes a psychologist and coach who filters out the needs in discussions, understands the personality of the employee, and thus supports him in his wishes and strengths. Sensitivity and empathy are most important at this level (more on this in the next section, "The Empathetic Psychologist").

In addition to these four methods, ensuring fairness in interpersonal communication on a daily basis, promoting entrepreneurial thinking and action among employees, and giving them more room for self-fulfillment and feeling good at work are *very* important. Do this "just because" it's the right thing, not for transactional reasons in return for good performance.

That way, employees feel that they do not have to earn the manager's appreciation first in order to feel good about their work. Rather, they have your appreciation right from the start.

This appreciation can be reflected in a wide variety of ways, such as:

- sincere praise and gratitude, without linking them to achievements;

- surprises, like pizza, without tying them to performance;

- coaching or mentoring by the manager himself;

- joint target definitions in which the employee has an equal say;

- positive language and words of encouragement when things are not going well for the employee;

- a positive error culture;

- a strong feedback culture;

- free and healthy snacks and drinks at the workplace;

- a humorous approach;

- free continuing education for employees;

- modern working environment, especially the latest work tools and tech; and

- a high degree of independence (regulating their work hours themselves, being able to decide on and implement plans).

This list is far from exhaustive, of course, but it conveys the general idea that promoting a good work atmosphere leads to increased enjoyment of work and employees being happy to get up in the morning to go to the office in the first place—all very beneficial in the long run. And it's precisely the globally hated Monday that shows how most companies are still a long way from implementing these ideas.

Of course, not all organizations have as much money as Google or Apple and can turn the workplace into a theme park of productivity. But that's not the point. If your organization doesn't make millions in sales, then no employee expects four weeks of free vacation and his own office with a view of Central Park in New York. But every employee senses whether the manager is making an effort within his means. That's what matters most; it's the genuine effort that counts.

The impact of successful transformational leadership can hardly be overestimated. In a positive work and communication environment, it's not only the employee's performance that increases. His identification with the company, his work satisfaction, his dealings with customers, and the daily inner commitment to the organization—all of these will increase as a result of transformational leadership in a positive environment. All in all, those are some pretty good reasons to at least try it.

EXERCISE #18: And now you!

Consider which of the above points regarding transactional leadership you can implement within your financial means. Make a plan, and follow through.

A final thought: You might now ask yourself whether transactional and transformational leadership are mutually exclusive. The first is based on the principle of exchange, relying on extrinsic factors, while the second is based on a positive ideology, relying more on intrinsic ones. And the answer here is very pragmatic: If you're not getting anywhere with an employee with one of these two leadership styles, then just try a different leadership style. In order to know which leadership style and method suit which employee, you, as a manager, must also be a good judge of character. And this is exactly what the following chapter is about.

Personality Types & Team Building

Chapter overview:

01. Personality types according to the 4-color model
02. The performance review as the key to the employee
03. Effective team building measures

At first glance, the title "The Empathetic Psychologist" might seem a bit strange. Correctly assessing the character, building trust, recognizing strengths and boosting self-confidence in others—these are typical tasks of a psychologist and coach. But it also helps you as a manager if you can correctly assess the employee's character and learn to speak his language, so to speak. Being a coach means, first of all, knowing personality types and how to conduct which employee interview or performance review to achieve the best possible result.

01 Personality types according to the 4-color model

There are many personality models that try to categorize people and describe their personality in a simplified way. Particularly popular in Europe, for example, are the DISG model, the Myers-Briggs Type Indicator, the Enneagram, the Golden Personality Profiler, the Bochum Inventory for Job-Related Personality Description, the Giessen Test, and many others. Science doesn't think much of any of the previously mentioned, though. The prevailing opinion today speaks highly of the OCEAN model, which assesses people in five categories (Openness, Conscientiousness, Extraversion, Agreeableness, Neuroticism).

In general, all personality models start from different premises and place different weight on different factors. You can simply take any online personality test (just google it) as a small experiment to get a first impression. But this book is not intended to be a summary of personality tests; rather, it offers practical, specific tools that you can apply immediately.

So, in the following, I would like to introduce you to a simple model that you can immediately apply to your employees and have successful conversations with the respective personality type: the *4-color model*, which is strongly based on the DISG model. According to the model, a distinction is made between red, blue, yellow, and green types.

Before we get started, a quick question first: Why is it actually so important to master type-appropriate communication? Very simple. Let's imagine that the boss praises an employee who really doesn't need any praise and just wants a raise. The boss didn't need to praise him. Or vice versa: Imagine that an employee wants nothing more than praise from her supervisor. And what does he get? A written notice of a salary increase. However, this does not make the employee happy right now. As you can see from these two small examples, the same behavior can have a completely different effect. It's therefore very beneficial and makes more sense to give the employee the right thing at the right time.

a) The red type

The red type of person is dominant, decisive, and impatient. He frequently interrupts other people, is always in a hurry, and wants to see results quickly. He is full of energy, very driven, and doesn't shy away from conflict. He communicates his wishes and goals confidently and loves challenges. If he doesn't get the latter, he quickly gets bored. He likes it when you are efficient and don't beat around the bush but get straight to the point.

With this type of person, you don't need to spend a lot of time justifying and convincing. Instead, you need to succinctly formulate what needs to be done and when. The clearer, the better. Friendliness is usually a waste of time for the red type. He also expects you as a leader to be decisive, confident, and straightforward—just like him.

b) The blue type

The blue type of person loves to reflect and analyze all numbers, data, and facts before making a decision. He's no stranger to intensive thought processes. He is always well prepared and punctual. He likes to think a lot, in other words, so he often seems somewhat aloof and introverted to others.

The best way to convince him is through good, factual arguments, logical thought processes, and relevant examples. He quickly recognizes errors and always listens with scrutiny and attention. His best friend is precision. If you have such a person in front of you, prepare the facts well and stay factual. He doesn't have much use for emotion, though. So score points with objectivity, calmness, and rationality.

c) The yellow type

The yellow type of person is very sociable and interested in people. He enjoys listening to stories, telling anecdotes, and making others laugh. He is super connected and almost always in a good mood. He is creative, communicative, and extroverted.

The yellow type also likes to talk about private things and seeks and needs recognition from his colleagues and from you as a manager. Due to his large circle of acquaintances and his desire to please everyone, he is not the best person for getting things done. He is also easily influenced by what others say. On the other hand, he's optimistic and creates a good atmosphere in the team. With the yellow type, take time to build the relationship and make sure to be like him: positive, open, and talkative.

d) The green type

The green type of person loves harmony. He is very empathetic, emotional, and would rather avoid conflicts. He is reliable and valued for her loyalty, but because he avoids conflict, he is not very assertive. He is too quickly satisfied with compromise in the spirit of harmony.

As an honest and trustworthy person, he expects you to trust him and value his feelings. He is also a good team player, so it's important to him that the decisions you communicate are also a good fit for the entire team and are fair. Above all, with the green type, be understanding and do not create conflicts.

e) Using the 4-color model in everyday work life

These four types of people are ideal or easily definable types. In reality, all four elements come out in people to a greater or lesser extent. But usually one color dominates. And what that color is, of course, you'll find out in a detailed performance review (more on that in the next section).

> **EXERCISE #19: Putting your employees under the magnifying glass**
>
> Think about what personality type each of your employees is, and in your conversations with them, make sure that you communicate in a more type-appropriate way from now on. It's best to make a small list for this right away and keep track of everything.

Of course, the 4-color model is a strong simplification of the human psyche. But this classification draws attention to something very important. Namely, you should be a different leader for each type of person, adapt to that type, and ask yourself carefully before each performance review: **What does my employee need most?** If you incorporate this realization into your everyday work life, it's a big win for you. Most managers have their singular "style" and are the same to all employees. Sure, this is consistent, but it's less promising. You won't get far with the yellow type with numbers, data, and facts, for example. You'll just annoy the blue type with small talk.

At this point, I am often asked by executives in coaching sessions: *"But is it still authentic if I completely adapt to the other person's personality?"* That's a very good question, too!

Matching the other person is not about absolute matching, like a clone. You don't have to change your entire character. Of course, you have a core behavior with which you're 100% in the comfort zone. There's the outer sphere, too, which makes you feel completely uncomfortable (see illustration). But there's also an in-between area where you can meet the employee part way without feeling inauthentic. And it is precisely this area we're talking about. Build flexibility here to the extent that seems reasonable to you.

A small personal example of this: I don't like small talk. And yet, I often have yellow clients who like to make small talk at the beginning of coaching and feel more comfortable as a result. What do I do? I of course don't break up the small talk and say: *"Let's get right to it, please!"* Instead, I join in on the small talk a bit, even if I don't like it. I then slowly but surely lead us over to the exercises, and the actual coaching can begin. So, it's a slight adjustment that strengthens the relationship between you and the other person—that's my job as a coach, and it's your job as a leader. Here we are in the middle circle of the figure above.

When does this kind of empathetic communication play a very crucial role? During the performance review, of course! Enough with the small talk and let's get right to it.

02 The performance review

The performance review is one of the core tasks of the manager. First, a well-structured performance review strengthens the **relationship** between you and your employee. Second, you and the employee can **analyze the past** in this conversation. Third, you can give each other **feedback** about what went well and what didn't. Fourth, the review is also about defining **goals for the future**. Fifth and final, it's about the path and **milestones** to get there. That's a lot of demands resting on a single conversation.

This list is not even exhaustive. But already from these five points you can see that it is too much for a single conversation. If you take the five points very seriously, then it's too much even for two conversations. Unfortunately, there is a habit among managers in many countries to hold the performance review only once or twice a year. No wonder that both employees and managers are dissatisfied with the results. That's a lot of time in between reviews! If you try to address everything, it becomes superficial. And if you pick out two or three points, you've probably left out some important issues.

My clear recommendation is to conduct a detailed review at least once a month. This has the simple advantage that you always remain up to date with the employee and can intervene immediately in the event of undesirable developments. That way, months don't go by before you realize together at the annual meeting in December that things haven't been going well since September.

The frequent review is also about a well-prepared guideline and creating a pleasant atmosphere.

a) The performance review setting

You should allow sufficient time for the interview (at least one hour) and communicate the planned time frame to the employee beforehand. It makes sense, as with any meeting, to prepare a small agenda of what the meeting will be about. The employee should also be given the opportunity to integrate his own topic points. That way, both of you know exactly what the review is about before it starts, and you're both prepared for it. As a rule of thumb, you should put the same amount of time into preparing the review as you think it will take (i.e., 1 hour review = 1 hour of prep time).

And now the common response: *"What? I'm supposed to spend a whole two hours on a performance review? Per month? Per employee?"*

Many managers don't want to take that much time for an employee. And that's plain wrong. The performance review is one of the most effective leadership tools you can use to positively influence an employee's behavior and attitudes. Your job is to lead people, not just have all the time to yourself to get only your tasks done.

Besides planning an agenda, you should also ensure a pleasant atmosphere. That doesn't just mean snacks and drinks. Start with some pleasant small talk (you'll have to cut it off if it's a yellow or green personality type!), or get right to the relevant points in a calm but efficient manner (for the red or blue types). Be conscious throughout the conversation of what each character type needs and how he wants to be guided and nurtured. Don't forget: Your own phone calls and other interruptions are taboo during the interview phase. The employee should know that he's your top priority for the next hour.

And now to the individual topics of the performance review:

b) Criticize correctly

In my job as a business coach, I give feedback every day. Feedback is my most important tool. It's also the main reason why clients come to me: to get excellent feedback. But giving excellent feedback is an art in itself. And while we all know that criticism should be constructive, most people have a hard time phrasing it in a way that the other person can accept the feedback. I thus present some very important tips to help you give the right feedback.

The first rule of feedback is: Match the rigor of your feedback to the employee's maturity level. What exactly does that mean? It describes the fact that new employees are rather insecure, so a hypercritical and 100% honest feedback makes them very uncomfortable. They end up performing even worse because they're even more afraid of making mistakes. For new employees, for example, feedback should clearly state the mistakes and areas for improvement but in very gentle language. You're full of understanding for their inexperience and mix in a good pinch of praise. That way, the inexperienced employee can carefully build self-confidence and trust himself to do more in the future.

Conversely, employees with a high level of maturity and experience enjoy negative feedback— because they know they are good and don't need constant adulation; they want to know what they can work on right away. Negative feedback should be presented in a factual and respectful manner no matter what. That way, employees can more easily accept it. Professionals always want to improve and will be grateful to you for even the smallest recommendation because it will lift them to an even higher level of performance. Every now and then, politicians or rhetorically well-trained board members come to me and book several sessions or even block off the whole day to work on the finer points. These very good candidates should be told that they are already well above average and can only improve this and that by degrees.

However, most employees are neither absolute beginners nor absolute professionals, but are somewhere in the middle. So it's natural, then, that praise and criticism should be more or less balanced for average employees. And it's best not to give the feedback intuitively or spontaneously. Instead, as you prepare for the review, take the time to note down five points that went well and five points that should go better.

Especially at critical points, the employee will often try to justify himself immediately. Everyone wants to defend himself when attacked. Mark Twain's irony hits the nail on the head here:

> "I like criticism, but it must be my way."

But you can make the critical feedback more acceptable if you pay attention to the following criteria.

- **Be analytical**: If you find something that needs correcting, use reasons and examples to substantiate your negative criticism. The behavior triangle is excellent for this purpose. First, describe the *situation* you want to talk about, then the employee's *action*, and third, the *result.* In this way, you ensure that the fault you find in the employee's behavior is explained in a logical and comprehensible manner.

- **Be precise**: Of course, you should describe the situation, action, and result as precisely as possible. You should also define quite precisely what you find fault with.

- **Be solution-oriented**: You should have at least one solution or alternative ready for the employee on how to approach a similar situation in the future. People love solutions.

- **Be timely**: Of course, feedback should be provided as promptly as possible (i.e., while the employee is still 100% aware of the process and his behavior). If something major has gone wrong, don't wait until the end of the month. Talk to him right away.

- **Show respect**: The wording itself can also be problematic. For example, you should avoid strongly emotionally charged terms, such as "stupid" or "unbearable." These terms personally attack, condemn, and hurt the employee, even if you didn't mean it that way.

Giving feedback is enormously important. But it is no less important to receive feedback, i.e., to actively ask the employee what you as a manager can do better. If the employee is silent on this, encourage her to name at least one thing. Let's face it: Every employee finds fault with the boss. And if he doesn't say anything, it's just because he's afraid of you. Take away that fear by pointing out that you can't possibly do everything right either and need feedback to be a better leader.

Then, if the employee is brave and names a few things, one of the most important feedback rules is not to justify yourself. And definitely don't interrupt him. Interposed questions are of course allowed but should not sound like you're offended. They're purely informative.

After receiving the critical feedback, thank the employee. Even if you do not agree with the criticism and have good arguments, don't refute the employee. That would only result in the employee not saying anything negative the next time. They'd be afraid that you can't accept criticism anyway, so why bother trying it again?

c) Praise correctly

Let's take my country of residence as an example. Is Germany a good example of a culture of praise? Well, let me tell you. There's about as much praise in German companies as there is water in a desert. Two-thirds of employees in Germany receive praise from their supervisor only once a month, or even less. Approximately 70 days elapse between two positive feedbacks. A catastrophic value! Most managers (and not just German ones, now) think they praise enough, even though the absolute majority of workers would like more frequent praise. What's going wrong here?

Praising someone and recognizing their achievements is actually not that difficult. And it costs nothing. Yet most managers don't do it. Benjamin Franklin offers some good advice on this regard:

> "When you're good to others, you're best to yourself."

And that's saying a lot, Someone who's mediocre himself has probably rarely received genuine praise in his life. That makes it particularly difficult for him to hand out much praise at all; he's too focused on himself. Because the thought process is: I was almost never praised myself, so why should I praise others?

Yet it requires inner greatness to honestly acknowledge the achievements of others. Even if you find praising others difficult for personal reasons, remember the motivating effect of praise. It not only makes you feel better too, in the end. Many studies have shown that praise motivates employees and makes them want to do more, be more productive. Just think of Dan Ariely's "pizza study" described earlier. Praise from the boss is worth even more to many people than praise from a life partner.

Nowadays, too, many people don't just work to survive, but to achieve self-fulfillment. If you rarely or never receive praise for your work, this chips away at your self-esteem eventually. And that, in turn, reduces motivation to work hard for your organization.

Praise expressed in person has the most impact. But even a handwritten note or a short email pleases the employee; a quick phone call is great too. Don't overdo it with praise, it goes without saying. Too much of it quickly comes across as contrived and no one buys it. But don't forget: Praise more than just once a month!

d) Analyze the past

The exact words for praise and criticism, including these tips, aren't just floating around the room, ready-made. They're specifically applied when you review the past in the performance review and analyze, from your perspective, what went well and what didn't go well. The analysis of the past is concerned, first of all, with the "hard" questions of target achievement. Secondly, it's about "soft" questions relating to job satisfaction.

But what questions are best for analyzing the past? Take a look below to find 20 question ideas for your next performance review. Of course, you can add your own questions to these two question lists. The point of them is to be aware of the balance between issues of fact and issues of feeling; you're not just looking at the numbers that have been achieved.

Here is a selection of ten good **factual questions**:

- What goals from the last performance review were not met / met / exceeded?
- How do you evaluate the past period since the last review?
- Are there any issues that should be resolved as soon as possible? What are the causes of these problems?
- When are there delays in workflows and how could they be reduced?
- Which projects have you been particularly successful with?
- In which tasks would you need more support and in what form?
- What do you think we should do differently? What can I do and what can the company do better? Do you have any specific suggestions for me?
- What could you work on more intensively next year? And which tasks do you think deserve less effort and time?
- In your view, is the internal and external communication right?

- Are there specific work tools we should acquire to make your job easier?

And here is a selection of ten good **state-of-mind questions**:

- Where are there currently dead ends, and where would you like to see more support?
- What currently bothers you about your job?
- What is your favorite thing to work on?
- Do you find your current work challenging, or not challenging enough?
- How is the teamwork going? Is there any potential for conflict?
- How satisfied are you in your job at the moment?
- What can I do to increase your satisfaction?
- What would you like to work on more in the future?
- What continuing education courses would you like to take? How could you incorporate the acquired knowledge into your daily work?
- Are there still points that I have not addressed but you'd very much like to talk about?

Especially the state-of-mind questions (for finding out what your employee's state of mind is, of course) help you find out more about the employee's true interests and motivations. You already know from the section on successful negotiation that good questions are the most important tool for finding out what the employee really thinks, what interests him, and what bothers him.

Don't fire off too many questions in a row. You don't want the employee feeling like he's being interrogated, but do throw in the odd question or two during natural conversation. It's also important not to be satisfied with a short answer. Use follow-up and definition questions to get at what the employee really means. Sometimes only these follow-up questions bring the employee's true state of mind to light. But that's exactly what you want.

e) Agree on goals and milestones

As far as goal definition is concerned, the SMART formula presented in the chapter "The Effective Manager" is ideal. The formulated goals should be specific, measurable, attractive, realistic and timed. The same applies to milestones. Prioritizing goals (there's always more than one) and roughly defining the amount of time required for each is also important.

The goals I'm talking about here include performance goals and behavior goals, i.e., not only what the employee is supposed to achieve, but also what behavior or methods he can use to achieving it. In the spirit of situational leadership, it's advisable to give employees with a relatively low level of maturity as much direction as possible. Employees with a high level of maturity can make suggestions for goals and their implementation as independently as possible, since they usually have their priorities in order already, know what needs to be tackled first.

Now, a quick word about agreeing on targets: Clearly defined (realistic and easy-to-follow) numbers provide clarity and objectivity at a glance. Unfortunately, some managers set their goals too high out of false ambition. That naturally leads to performance pressure and stress for the employee. How realistic the achievement of objectives is for the specific employee therefore plays a crucial role in agreeing on them.

In industries with rapidly changing circumstances, there is also a constant need to completely overturn goals and define new ones. But even if you realize only later that the goals set in the performance review were set incorrectly, it's best to sit down with the employee again immediately.

Finally, it's important not only to define *quantitative* goals, i.e. those that can be easily measured. Classic examples of quantitative targets are quarterly sales, number of contracts concluded or number of goods manufactured. It's also vital to define *qualitative* goals—such as better teamwork or higher customer satisfaction— even if these cannot be measured objectively. By including certain topics in the target agreement, you encourage the employee to actively focus on these things and, for example, make more of an effort to produce higher customer satisfaction, optimize his behavior towards that goal. To ensure that the employee can best concentrate on the jointly defined goals and milestones, there shouldn't be too many of them. Less is more, as far as achievable goals are concerned.

EXERCISE #20: Review the goals for your employees

Have you defined qualitative goals in addition to quantitative ones? Have you applied the SMART formula? When defining the goals, did you differentiate according to the maturity level of the respective employee? Analyze your employee's established goals and correct them together with your employee in an upcoming performance review.

f) Common assessment errors by managers

Of course, performance reviews are about the evaluation of the employee's performance. And as with any human evaluation, very specific cognitive biases play a role in clouding your judgment. This is both annoying for the employee, who may (rightly!) feel unfairly judged. And it's not right for you to make a biased judgment about an employee either, since you're interested in arriving at a correct judgment, something that helps him improve. Here are the five most common cognitive biases you should pay close attention to when reviewing employees:

- **Halo effect**: The halo effect refers to the psychological fact that people infer from a known positive characteristic (e.g. good looks) that other, unknown characteristics are positive too. The positive quality outshines the whole personality, glowing like a halo over the person being judged. Tip: Don't be blinded by a positive trait; evaluate the employee's strengths and weaknesses independently.

- **Horn effect**: The horn effect describes exactly the opposite of the halo effect. One negative trait puts a damper on all other traits of an employee, so no matter how well he has performed, he will always be seen in a bad light. The tip above for dealing with the halo effect also applies here (evaluate strengths and weaknesses independently).

- **Primacy effect**: The primary effect describes the fact that people are very strongly influenced by first impressions. So, if an employee made a mess of the first project of the year but then brought another three projects to a good conclusion, the first project sticks out in our memory, shaping our perception of the person. Tip: Don't be fooled by a first impression! Look for consistent good work.

- **Recency effect**: The recency effect describes exactly the opposite phenomenon. We are disproportionately influenced by the last impression someone makes. For example, the last project of the year went wrong and makes you forget about the employee's previous good work. Tip: Don't be fooled by a last impression either! Consider all of the employee's work.

- **Similarity-attraction effect**: This effect describes the tendency to find people more likable who are similar to yourself, whether they talk similarly, have similar ideas, or have similar ways of working. These are the people you prefer quite unconsciously. But, of course, many roads lead to Rome. Your own way of working is not necessarily the best. Tip: Accept other work styles as well and realize that employees who tick completely differently than you can still do excellent work, and they'd like to be appreciated for it!

It's best to consciously pay attention to these cognitive biases and come to an unclouded judgment of your employee. If you're interested in learning more about other cognitive distortions and manipulations and how they can be used, I recommend my online course "Tricks of Trump: His best Manipulation Techniques".

g) Regular (constant) performance reviews

We have looked at a lot of topics and a lot of questions for the performance review. But I do stress that it's important not to overload a conversation with too many topics. You can achieve this by scheduling regular employee reviews, not leaving them to once a year. And even if you feel like there's really nothing to talk about, have a review anyway. Even if you don't have any issues, it's quite possible the employee does. And if the employee himself does not have a specific reason, you can exchange ideas noncommittally in a pleasant atmosphere, which strengthens the relationship level between you and your employee.

03 Team building

Team building describes the process of employees growing together into a mutually supportive team, where everyone fights not only for themselves, but also for each other. There are two starting points for this: the topic of what binds existing teams together, and the topic of what you should look for in new recruits.

a) Team events for bonding

Everyone knows about the extraordinary things employees do that are supposed to foster team spirit: paintball, bowling, cooking class, skiing, hiking, climbing, eating steak, barbecuing, running marathons, archery, soccer tournaments, foosball tournaments, quiz shows, rafting, curling—there's nothing the team can't do together, apparently!

These types of events strengthen team spirit, the providers claim. That's not entirely wrong, sure. Events like this can be fun and you get to see a very personal side of your colleagues and bosses. But the effect of such events fizzles out relatively quickly.

Team building should therefore take place primarily *at* work. What can you do about it? You can make sure that ...

- ... you clearly communicate the goal towards which the team is working;

- ... the team is the right size (especially not too big, so everyone knows one another);

- ... the team is involved in weekly and monthly planning;

- ... there is a fair method of communication;

- ... everyone is allowed to finish;

- ... not everything is done individually;

- ... first signs of bullying are dealt with and prevented in the future;

- ... employees can come to you if there are any problems;

- ... regular meetings, such as group lunch breaks exist, where employees can relax when not working;

- ... employees can take coffee breaks together and talk about private matters;

- ... successes are celebrated together;

- ... team workshops are held where employees can further their education together as a team;

- ... colleagues are explicitly made aware of being able to ask each other for help; and

- there should be regular team meetings to consider together how to work more intensively as a team.

You can implement many of these points on a daily basis to foster a better team spirit. Great external company events, like bowling, are a nice bonus from time to time. But the focus should be on your commitment to team spirit at work, today, every day. There is always something to do in the spirit of good teamwork at work.

b) Strategic recruiting

A huge part of team building is also recruiting. New hires bring in personalities that may not fit the team right away; they have to integrate slowly. To ensure that this process runs as smoothly as possible, it's important when recruiting new employees to make sure that there's a *cultural fit*, i.e., that the new employee not only fits in terms of qualifications, but also in terms of his values and work ethic.

For you, this means explicitly focusing on corporate culture during interviews, asking the applicant what he thinks of your corporate values. If he says something inadequate or inappropriate, then move on. Psychological research has long since found that one misfit or negative employee is enough to drag down the performance of the entire team. Whether through bullying, bad temper, mean comments, self-important posturing or taking advantage of help from colleagues—employees are usually powerless against a colleague's antisocial behavior, and this naturally depresses everyone. So, when recruiting, pay close attention to the applicant's social profile and don't let the bad apple join the team in the first place.

And if conflicts should arise among employees anyway, you, as a manager, should be more than capable of solving them. That's what the fifth role of the leader is all about: the Skilled Problem Solver.

Conflict Management & Change Management

Chapter overview:

01. Professional conflict management
02. Professional change management

01 Professional conflict management

Any standard English dictionary would do, but it's interesting to look specifically at the German dictionary's definition (Duden) of "conflict" as

> a difficult situation created by a clash of conflicting views, interests, or the like, which may lead to discord.

Important in this definition is the little word "may": Not every conflict necessarily leads to discord or a falling out. So if you get it right, as a manager, you can resolve most conflicts—or even better: prevent them entirely.

Before we really get started, one more important thought: Most people associate the word "conflict" with negative connotations such as strife, anger, threat, burden, escalation, defeat, struggle, loss of face, loss of trust, etc. But all those words represent only one way of looking at conflict. Conflict can also be seen as an opportunity and an impetus for change. Almost every conflict leads to an inner or outer change. And that, if handled properly, can lead to an improvement in how things work from now on at the office. But enough context. Let's get right into conflict management!

a) What types of conflict are there?

It is helpful to distinguish between the different types of conflict. That way, you can better know how to deal with each one. Here are the eight most common types of conflict.

- **Conflict of goals**: Two or more people who are dependent on one another pursue different goals that interfere with or exclude each other.

- **Conflict of means**: Two or more people disagree on what means should be used to achieve a goal, although the goal might be the same.

- **Conflict of values**: Different value systems (such as religion, political or world views) lead to friction between parties. The parties are inwardly convinced their value systems are the right ones, so derive different meaning or consequences from their actions (intercultural conflicts, for example, or conflicts between the old and new generations).

- **Conflict of roles**: These conflicts can exist between different roles (e.g. manager and employee), within a role (thinking about profit on the one hand, thinking about the welfare of an employee on the other) or due to ill-defined roles (keyword: "Who gets to do what when?").

- **Distribution conflict**: The parties argue about the distribution of available but limited resources (monetary, technical, symbolic, etc.).

- **Relationship conflict**: At least one of the parties feels a personal antipathy or rejection towards the other person, without necessarily knowing the reason for it.

- **Power conflict**: The typical struggle within a group for alpha status or being the top person (also called status conflict).

- **Change conflict**: When members, roles or norms change within an existing structure, and parts of the group do not agree with the change (more on this in the sub-chapter "Change Management").

So, if two are arguing, you first need to figure out what type of conflict it is. In doing so, you should not look at the positions (i.e. what is said), but at the underlying motivations and interests of the conflicting parties, as already described above in the section on conducting successful negotiations. It's also very useful to know the different conflict personalities.

b) What are the conflict personalities?

Not everyone behaves the same within a conflict type. In general, four conflict personalities can be distinguished:

- **The competitive type**: He sees conflict as a battle in which only one can prevail and walk away victorious. For him, conflict is a zero-sum game and he will do anything to come out on top. In other words, he is also not afraid to harm the other party if it means he'll achieve victory.

- **The selfish type**: This conflict personality thinks first and foremost of himself. In contrast to the competitive type, the selfish type can also consider the interests of the other parties if it doesn't harm his own advantage.

- **The selfless/defensive type**: This conflict personality thinks first of the interests of others. As soon as a conflict is brewing, this guy waves the white flag and immediately avoids tough disputes, even at the cost of personal disadvantage.

- **The cooperative type**: With him, justice is the absolute. He doesn't just want a fair solution but a long-term solution that is profitable for both sides, enabling long-term cooperation.

These four conflict personalities mean that there are four different ways of dealing with conflict.

EXERCISE #20: Your own conflict personality

Consider what conflict personality you represent and, if you are not the cooperative type, what inner beliefs prevent you from always approaching conflict in the spirit of cooperation.

c) What are the types of conflict resolution?

When two competitive types collide, **confrontation** is inevitable. In this first path to conflict resolution, neither party wants to back down. Everyone wants to win and enforce his position 100%. In this case, the one who holds the more powerful position, or the one who pretends to be more powerful to the other, usually prevails. This happens too when the competitive type and the selfish type clash and the latter can find no common interests.

When the competitive type meets the selfless/defensive type, conflict resolution proceeds along the path of **adaptation** or **avoidance**. The selfless/defensive type doesn't want to deal with the conflict and simply conforms to the dictates of the competitive type (and the selfish type). The same happens, of course, when two defensive types collide.

The third way of conflict management often takes place between egoistic conflict types. If they mutually recognize that they cannot enforce their positions because they realize it's a problem of hierarchy, for example, then they try to **compromise**. They make concessions and, pragmatic as they are, they achieve at least part of the goals they set.

Finally, the fourth way of conflict resolution: **cooperation**. The cooperative type tries to come up with a win-win solution no matter the conflict personality. He tries (intuitively, or consciously, following the Harvard concept presented above) to find out the underlying interests and strives for a fair resolution to the conflict in which both sides benefit and want to keep cooperating.

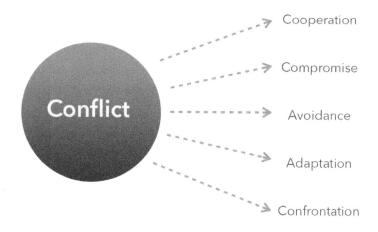

If the people involved use a third party to manage the conflict, then conflict **moderation** and **mediation** (conflict management by an independent third party without decision-making authority) and **voluntary jurisdiction** and **legal action** (conflict management by an independent third party with decision-making authority) are added as types of conflict management.

But cooperation, i.e. the Harvard approach, is truly the magic number because through cooperation, the parties involved are most satisfied when both come out of the conflict as winners. But for that to happen, you have to be very well prepared for the conflict situation.

d) Communicative conflict amplifiers

What do I mean by this, exactly? It sounds more complex than it actually is. The causes of conflicts are extremely varied, as is already evident from the different types of conflict (see above). And there are countless other causes for conflicts, such as fear, thinking about status, there being too many people involved, too little time, individual differences in perception, prejudices, and lack of acceptance, and, and, and ...

What all causes of conflict have in common, however, are communicative errors (amplifiers) that one or more participants commit, consciously or unconsciously. These errors reinforce conflict over time.

15 Conflict Amplifiers

1. Making snide remarks about the other party.

2. Communicating only on the factual level, resulting in complete neglect of the relationship, self-revelation, and appeal levels.

3. Concealing or avoiding the real issue.

4. A party deliberately not saying what they mean.

5. Ambiguous communication of one's position.

6. If the other person doesn't understand but doesn't ask for clarification (out of politeness or shyness, for example), resulting in misunderstandings becoming greater over time.

7. One person talking a lot but hardly listening, and not asking questions.

8. Focusing on weak points to refute the other person, rather than highlighting the legitimate points, which are deliberately avoided (straw man technique).

9. Showing passive-aggressive behavior (aggression is communicate "through the nose").

10. Using derogatory body language and negative or provocative vocal delivery.

11. Using pompous, pretentious language.

12. Not being available, or being constantly absent.

13. Communicating an unwillingness to face the conflict at all.

14. Not showing face, literally (using emails instead of a face-to-face conversation).

15. Allotting too little time to be able to talk reasonably.

These communicative conflict amplifiers are rarely committed by only one party in the conflict. Usually, when the conflict has reached a certain stage of escalation, both sides start committing these errors in communication. In order not to inflame the conflict even further, it's important to avoid these 15 mistakes in your own communication. And, if the other person commits these communication sins, to point them out discreetly and kindly with the help of the mirror technique.

The *mirror technique*, if you recall, was already discussed in the subsection, "Be a team leader, be a group leader." To recap briefly: With this technique, you show the other person a metaphorical communication mirror, pointing out a particular communication mistake that he regularly makes (example: "Do you realize that you keep interrupting me?").

Now you know which linguistic subtleties you should pay attention to in a conflict situation. And now, of course, you might be wondering: How can I prepare for the conflict situation in terms of content?

e) How do you ideally prepare for conflict meetings?

There are a number of things you can prepare for before a conflict meeting. The good news is: It's always the same points you need to work on. Here's a checklist of questions you should answer for yourself before a conflict meeting:

Conflict Resolution Checklist

1. What type of conflict is it? (conflict of goals, values, methods, etc.).

2. Which conflict personality am I dealing with?
   (competitive type, selfish type, selfless type, or cooperative type).

3. Which way of conflict management do I want to choose?
   (confrontation, avoidance/adaptation, compromise, cooperation).

4. What is the possible cause of the conflict?

5. With which proposed solution do I enter the conflict situation?

6. What alternative do I have if I cannot solve the conflict with
   the other party?

7. What concessions can I make? And which not?

8. What motives and alternatives might the other party have?

9. What objections and accusations can be expected, and how do I respond to them?

10. How do I create a positive atmosphere? (privacy, snacks, small talk,
    no interruption, active listening, open body language, pleasant voice, look for
    common interests and values).

f) As a leader, what roles can you play in conflict management?

There are varying degrees of involvement with which you can approach a single conflict. The roles range from conflict resolution initiator (who merely initiates a conflict resolution process among employees) to conflict decider (who makes an independent decision that is binding for the employees). Here you'll find the possible degrees of involvement in conflict management:

- **Conflict resolution initiator**: Here, you suggest that two employees at odds should address the conflict themselves. As an initiator, your job already ends there. Both the processes for conflict resolution and the conflict resolution itself are worked out independently by the parties. This role is particularly useful when the conflict is in its early stages and the parties are still comfortable talking to each other.

- **Conflict advisor**: Here, too, you're not involved in the conflict management directly. You stand outside the parties' discussions, but you give them suggestions and tips if they wish, without intervening in the actual events. These can be mainly (confidential) one-on-one meetings, with one or more parties involved. This role is particularly useful if at least one of the parties in the conflict is at a loss for what to do and asks you for advice.

- **Conflict moderator**: Here, you moderate the conflict discussions and are actively involved in the resolution process. Your task is to create the perfect framework for conflict resolution, with the solution finally coming from the parties themselves. You moderate the discussions, ensure that rules are observed, and you're neutral, only intervening, for example, when things get heated. You also point out when irrelevant things are being discussed. This role is particularly useful when the conflicting parties are too emotionally involved to talk to each other alone and with reason.

- **Conflict mediator**: Similar to the moderator, the mediator is responsible for the process of resolution, while the parties are responsible for the content of the discussions. However, the mediator is more actively involved in the process than the moderator in that he can actively intervene in the clarification process by asking questions; he can also lead the discussions in an impartial manner. In contrast to neutrality (with the accompanying emotional distance), all-partiality means that the mediator identifies with all parties and consequently (if necessary) helps the party that is weaker in communication (at a given point in time) to articulate themselves better. Thus, the mediator is fundamentally neutral, but he may empathetically adapt his behavior to the given situation. By the way, anyone who steps up to the situation, as it were, may call himself a "mediator." However, if you want to do this professionally, I'd recommend mediation training. If the training meets the requirements of the German Mediation Act, you could receive the designation of "certified mediator" (§ 5 para. 2 MediationsG; if you're not working in Germany, check with your local employment and work regulator for any guidelines on workplace conflict mediation and mediation certification). You can also hire a professional mediator if you feel that you (would) not get anywhere on your own. This role is also particularly useful when the parties in the conflict are too emotionally involved to talk reasonably to each other and ask you to be more actively involved in managing the conflict.

- **Conflict manager**: Here, the role gets even bigger. The conflict manager's task is to analyze the conflict himself, develop concepts for conflict resolution, and directly support the parties in implementing the resolution. Three schools of conflict management have emerged in 20th century peace studies. **Conflict settlement** is about quickly resolving the conflict by finding result-oriented strategies that can be implemented quickly and without necessarily addressing the causes of the conflict. Thus, conflict settlement is about ending the "bloodshed" as quick as possible. Methods of conflict settlement include the manager "laying down the law" to just end it already, or negotiations in which a perhaps less than satisfying but nonetheless quick compromise is reached between the parties. **Conflict resolution** is about finding the causes of conflict and eliminating them in the long term to ensure lasting peace. Conflict resolution seeks to satisfy unmet and often unexpressed basic needs. The methods involved here are detailed conflict analyses and the fleshing out of hidden interests and fears of the parties. And you, as a manager, may play a leading or accompanying role in these detailed discussions. Permanently improved communication between the parties is also an explicit goal. Finally, **conflict transformation** is about reconciling the parties in addition to resolving the conflict and creating a permanently just state between them. This form of conflict management takes a long time to accomplish because it seeks to transform the parties' attitudes toward the conflict and each other. It fundamentally reforms the complex factors involved in the conflict, too. This role of the conflict manager is appropriate when the parties in the conflict are seeking real structural and/or cultural change, so the goal is to create a better state than existed before the conflict.

- **Conflict arbitrator**: While the conflict manager actively supports the parties, he doesn't actually have any decision-making authority. The arbitrator is given the authority by the parties themselves to decide which proposal should be chosen as a solution, since they themselves cannot agree on a solution. Of course, the role of the arbitrator requires mutual trust and in-depth knowledge of the conflict. This role is appropriate when the parties to the conflict want you to choose a solution for them, since they're having a hard time getting to one themselves.

- **Conflict decider**: The decider also knows the history of the conflict but has the formal authority (or consent of the parties) to independently develop a proposed solution, making a decision capable of ending the conflict. This role is, of course, appropriate if the parties to the conflict want you to not just prepare, but also make a decision (be judge, jury, and executioner, so to speak).

g) Practical tips for conflict moderation/mediation

Looking at this detailed overview of the options for conflict resolution, you naturally wonder "Which ones are most appropriate for me?" The answer: conflict moderation and mediation. But even more specifically: what exact steps help you address a conflict? The following is a clear, play-by-play recommendation on what to do when moderating a conflict.

The **first step** is to create transparency regarding the conflict resolution process. You define your role as a neutral person who will ensure an orderly discussion and, if desired, contribute your own views and suggestions for a solution. You can also make it clear at this stage that conflict is commonplace, and that conflict mediation is an opportunity to improve the status quo. In doing so, you radiate confidence that reaching a resolution is only a matter of time.

In the **second step**, you should learn the positions of the conflicting parties. In keeping with the Harvard concept, you know that the underlying interests are quite essential. So, after the parties have revealed their positions, it is your task as moderator or mediator to follow up on *why* the conflicting parties hold these positions.

The **third step** involves hashing out a collection of topics, i.e., discussing and trying to settle the points relevant to the respective parties. Ideally, you ask the parties in the conflict to prioritize their concerns so you know what matters most to them.

In the **fourth step**, you should work on finding some creative options for resolving the conflict. *Brainwriting* is recommended, in which each person—after learning about the other's core concerns—tries to independently develop proposed solutions. Afterwards, *brainstorming* is used to collect ideas and develop them further as a group. Only then can the selection of the best solution take place.

In the **fifth and final step**, you summarize the parties' agreement in writing and define the next implementation steps with them; in an ideal situation, you link them to concrete instructions for action and deadlines.

You increase your chances of success if you approach the conflicting parties in a neutral, open, and appreciative manner throughout all phases. Whether you propose your own solutions, support the party with weaker communication skills, or want to "sell" a particular solution in the interest of the company—this all depends on the individual case. The most important thing, however, is to make the conflicting parties feel that you are concerned about a fair solution.

If you cannot guarantee neutrality, or if at least one party does not consider you neutral, conflict moderation or mediation should be eliminated as an option altogether. The party that considers you biased will not be able to accept your conflict management, and you also run the risk of being drawn into the conflict. So, clarify with the parties in advance whether they consider you neutral—and hire an external mediator if necessary.

h) Special problem: Bullying

Workplace harassment or bullying is one of the biggest problems on the job. Millions of people are bullied at work every single day. The number depends on exactly how you define bullying, but no one will seriously deny that it is a cross-industry plague. So, what can you do as a leader to confront it?

First of all, it's important to understand that bullying is not a phenomenon between two employees, but a group phenomenon. There's the tough-guy bully who insults, teases, and provokes a single colleague. But in reality, this rarely happens without the complicity of other colleagues. Either the bullying takes place while other colleagues watch silently and do not intervene, or the perpetrator tells his colleagues how helpless his bullying victim was when he insulted him with this or that. Again, in most cases, there is at least one other colleague—usually the friend of the bully—who is in on it.

This already results in the **first anti-bullying tip** for you as a manager: At regular intervals (for example, twice a year), point out that bullying is a commonplace phenomenon in many departments and that, if an employee is affected by it or has heard about it, he should contact you to clarify the matter (and any information, even in anonymous form, is very welcome). You, as the manager, are also probably legally obligated to stop bullying; you probably have a duty of care under labor law (not just in Germany but most likely in your country too) for your employees. You should thus counter bullying with warnings and, in extreme cases, transfers and terminations.

The **second anti-bullying tip** is to keep an open ear for insulting, sexist, demeaning, and harassing comments in all meetings and discussions. If it ever happens, document the incident in detail, preferably in writing, and quickly schedule (before or after) a confidential discussion with the colleague who made the comments and the colleague who was attacked. Victims of bullying often suffer from sleep disorders, anxiety, stomach pain, eating disorders, depression, and many other negative psychological effects that can quickly lead to an overwhelming feeling of resignation. It's therefore in your very best interest to intervene immediately at the very first sign of suspected bullying. By the way, four out of five victims of bullying are women. This is why a women's representative (equity officer) makes a lot of sense in the workplace, especially in larger companies.

Often the one who has a higher position and nothing to fear is the one doing the bullying. And that, by its very nature, applies to managers. When managers bully, this is referred to as "bossing." And statistically speaking, every second bullying case involves a supervisor. Why do managers do this? The manager might be compensating for his own insecurity and inadequacy through such behavior, or he's (needlessly) trying to demonstrate his power.

The **third anti-bullying tip**: Do an honest self-analysis by jotting down on a piece of paper when you might have given objectionable criticism, ostracized an employee or colleague, or bad-mouthed them in front of the whole group. And if you have colleagues who are your friends, ask them if they have already noticed such behavior, and ask them to tell you, one-on-one, if you have ever miscommunicated.

Finally, note how it's possible that you as a (newly appointed) manager are being bullied too, which, in technical jargon, is called "staffing," i.e., bullying by staff .

Here is a **fourth anti-bullying tip** for you: A good conflict coach can quickly remedy the situation and show you effective ways to skillfully communicate against and counter bullying.

Bullying becomes relevant under labor law when the acts of bullying (i.e. hostility, humiliation and intimidation) occur repeatedly, extend over a longer period of time, and affect the personality or health of the person concerned. Individual aspects may also have criminal relevance and must be reported immediately (in particular for German law: insult, defamation, and slander, §§ 185–187 StGB (the German penal code; check your local employment or workplace regulator for guidelines and laws applicable to workplace harassment)). To sum it all up: As a manager, you should always take the issue of bullying seriously and tackle it decisively. Don't forget to take a look in the mirror yourself every now and then.

02 Professional change management

A natural result of conflict is change. And nowadays, the successful management of changes resulting from conflict is referred to as change management.

Change, and therefore conflicts over change are inevitable in companies. The environmental movement (for example) forces both large and small companies to constantly make internal changes in order to remain competitive. Digitalization, globalization, and the robotization of the economy are also, in general, huge drivers of change, bringing about necessary transformations in strategy, structure, and decision-making. Remember, change is inevitable. So, simply put: anyone who doesn't adapt to new environment won't be on the market in a few years.

a) The two tools of change management: Fear and hope

In general, there are two ways to make change management palatable to employees: the fear principle and the hope principle.

If you want to use the tool of fear, your job is to paint the image of the status quo as bleak as possible. That is, show the worst consequences of what will happen if your organization doesn't implement change, and back it up by showing a high probability that these bad consequences will actually happen.

When it comes to the fear principle, many managers make the mistake of not explaining these negative consequences in sufficient detail. They want to implement change for good reasons, after all, but they don't adequately share these good reasons with their employees. Instead, they simply announce their decision about the decided change, and that's it. But that's a missed opportunity to gain complete acceptance for the change.

If you opt for the hope principle, then the strategy is the opposite of the fear principle. The hope principle is about clearly demonstrating to employees that the status quo is shoddy compared to what the company could actually achieve. So, change is not only necessary, but desirable.

When it comes to using the hope principle, though, many managers make the mistake of not attributing the positive consequences clearly enough to the individual employees. The question must be answered: "What's in it for the employees?" If you manage to answer this question well, the motivation for change becomes crystal clear for the employees, i.e., everyone can see the clear benefits of change.

b) Why employees are mostly against change

Even if the leadership team has prepared arguments for change and communicates them clearly to employees, most employees could still be against the proposed change. Why is that, actually?

The answer is relatively simple, a general truth: It's hard for people to give up their routines and learn new things. It costs time and energy. And as we know, people always try to take the path of least resistance. An example? New software: Even if new software has 100 new functions and is 1,000 times clearer, employees are still against it at first.

While this is irrational from a management perspective, it's highly rational from an employee perspective. Just think: it took them years to get used to the old software, and now they have to relearn new keyboard shortcuts, get used to a new design, a different deep structure of the program—everything is new and different.

So, convincing employees of the benefits of new software via the fear or hope principle is only half the battle. You also need to empower them to implement that change as easily as possible. This means offering further training and workshops for getting to know new software, for example. One-on-one coaching should also be an option, as well as online tutorials and explainer videos. Nowadays, nobody likes to read a manual, and not everyone absorbs information the same way anyway. A video, on the other hand, works wonders in the 21st century: it's entertaining and easy on the eyes. In other words, it's not enough to just sell the idea well; you need to make it easy to implement, too. These are equally important factors for successful change.

c) How the manager benefits from employee skepticism

Now, in your preparation, you have thought carefully about how to sell the change (keyword: fear/hope), and you also have a clear implementation plan that makes change easy for your employees. And yet, you can't expect employees to jump for joy. People are creatures of habit. Anything tried and true takes precedence over anything new.

However, you can use this natural skepticism to your advantage. Let's face it: If you're a leader who has decided to make a change, then you've fallen in love with your idea. When fleshing out your new idea, you naturally have the benefits of the new idea in mind. That's normal. In psychology, it's referred to as *confirmation bias*: The manager explicitly looks for advantages for the new idea but neglects all points that speak against it. Self-criticism is difficult but self-affirmation is pleasant, which is why hardly anyone is safe from confirmation bias.

The advantage for you: your employees are not as enthusiastic about the new idea as you are. In other words, it's not their own idea, so they try to find weaknesses in it. Now, many managers make the mistake of not subjecting their change concept to criticism, or ignoring criticism in order to avoid admitting to weaknesses in their idea. This proves fatal for the acceptance of change, however, because no change process can escape reality. The reality: it's your employees who must implement your idea, so naturally they're going to have small changes and critiques on a daily basis. Your job is to integrate the skeptical feedback into the change process, not just listen to employees and call it a day. Make them part of change management. That way, your idea becomes a shared process and employees become an integral and motivated part of the change.

The active participation of employees and the resulting faster acceptance of the change process has a psychological foundation called the IKEA effect. The term originated from the fact that people value a furniture product more when they have helped to build it themselves. In terms of numbers, the increased appreciation of homemade IKEA furniture almost reaches the appreciation of a unique piece of furniture made by a craftsman. If we take this idea and apply it to the active participation of the employee through his feedback and suggestions for improvement to the change process, it means that the employee will better appreciate change if he's more involved in it.

d) The 8-step process for leading change, by John P. Kotter

One of the pioneers of change management is Harvard Professor John P. Kotter, who describes eight exact steps an organization must go through for successful change management. This model can serve as a good checklist for your next change process:

Step 1: Create a sense of urgency (through good arguments and clear statements).

Step 2: Build a guiding coalition (effective individuals welded together into a team that trusts each other and is trusted by others).

Step 3: Form a strategic vision and initiatives (define the goal of change as a vision, and describe the way in which it is to be achieved).

Step 4: Enlist a volunteer army (communicate your vision with a convincing presentation to get all employees on board).

Step 5: Enable action by removing barriers (enable employees to tackle the change head-on, especially through workshops).

Step 6: Generate short-term wins (even if they are rather small at the beginning, successes should be celebrated to show that the process of change is going in the right direction).

Step 7: Sustain acceleration (deep change takes a lot of time and energy, so don't rest on small successes).

Step 8: Institute change (only when the changes are firmly anchored in the corporate culture has the change management process been successful).

As you can see, change management has more to do with good communication than anything else. So, at the end of this book, we come full circle to the first role of the manager: the Convincing Communicator.

Now that you know the five leadership roles and the tasks and tools associated with them, it's time for a brief conclusion.

Self-motivation as the Key to Success

The German author and philosopher Johann Wolfgang von Goethe once wrote:

> "One virtue above all others is the constant striving upwards, the wrestling with oneself, the insatiable desire for greater purity, wisdom, goodness, and love."

What Goethe unfortunately did not reveal is how exactly you get into this constant state of striving, how you can motivate yourself permanently. A takeaway from this quote is:

Everyone needs a good reason to get up in the morning and get going, full of energy and in a great mood.

So, in order to get into a high energy state yourself and achieve daily motivation, you need an attractive vision. But the million-dollar question is: What is a "good reason"? Top job? Recognition? An annual salary of $500,000?

Here's a very important insight: We have a good reason or a good vision when both the journey and the end result count, not just either or. So an attractive goal is not good enough; you have to really enjoy the nitty-gritty it takes to get there.

Think about it: If you only have the beautiful goal in mind but hate the road you're on, there might be some motivation, but there's no **lasting** motivation. In other words, every dull day eats up a little bit of your initial motivation until there is nothing left of it.

The problem most people have is that they get trapped in thinking about the future:

"When I can earn $500,000, then I'll truly be happy!"

"If I'm a Managing Director, then I'll know I've really made it!"

"I need to become a partner in the firm—then I'll really feel free."

There are two disadvantages to thinking about the future this way: First, reaching the goal is not guaranteed. After all, not every hard-working executive will also become the Managing Director or earn $500,000. You may work incredibly hard to become Managing Director, but then the salary might not match what you had in mind. What then?

The second disadvantage of thinking about the future this way is the realization that achieving not only Managing Director, but guaranteeing that big salary too—assuming that it works out—takes many, many years. So even if you've reached a certain dream salary after 30 years, you've lived those 30 years working like a dog, sacrificing your free time on the altar of your career.

It's important to understand that by staking your happiness on huge, career-driven goals, you're sacrificing the very best time of your life for something very distant and potentially unachievable. In reality, your life is being lived now, in every moment: You might wake up one day wondering, "Where'd all the time go?", wishing you could do something new that your old age now, unfortunately, doesn't permit.

You've probably heard of how, when people are asked shortly before they die what they regret most, the two most common answers are: *"I wish I had spent more time with friends/family"* and *"I wish I hadn't worked so much."* No one says at the end of his days: *"I wish I had spent more hours in the office!"* That should definitely make you think about your career vision and goals.

The consequence of this is clear: Each person's task is to construct a vision in which he also enjoys the individual steps along the way until the goal is achieved—meaning, you should enjoy the activity for itself and yet also feel the creative drive to keep going. Even if you were never able to reach your final goal, you would have felt joy and happiness in doing the work along the way.

These three drivers of motivation will help you greatly increase your self-motivation: autonomy, growth, and contribution.

The first driver—autonomy: Managers have much more creative freedom than regular employees and can therefore define their own professional vision more easily. This feeling of autonomy and self-determination gives managers inner freedom and desire to actively shape their work life. Think about it: Those who feel externally determined and perceive themselves as "cogs in the system" will hardly feel intrinsic motivation. Every person's desire for freedom is great—but those who truly feel free can also develop self-motivation more easily.

The second driver—growth: Every person has a natural urge to become better. If you always do the same thing and work through things according to a pattern, you will never develop further; you'll always remain where you are. Growth and getting better are forces built into us that we should use and tap into to become better. Again, managers tend to have more options than ordinary employees because they are much more in control of their own growth. They can make strategic decisions and have exclusive training, including more financial and corporate knowledge.

The third driver—contribution: There's this nice story about when John F. Kennedy once encountered a janitor at NASA with a broom and asked him what his job was. The janitor replied, *"I'm helping put a man on the moon."* You see, it's not so important how much money someone gets or what status someone has. If you're working on an idea that inspires you, that's a thousand times more important than a big salary. Or put another way: The job satisfaction of a top lawyer earning $190,000 a year and working 80 hours a week can be much lower than that of a web developer who gets $40,000 a year in an innovative start-up and works on a vision for a better world. And here, too, managers have a more favorable starting position for successful self-motivation compared to employees. This is because they determine what kind of contribution the entire company (or at least their department) should make—and the individual employees support them in this.

You can use these three drivers to increase your self-motivation without getting distracted by too many other options. In other words, let them have as high an impact as possible in your work life: Move aside anything in your work that might stand in the way, and let the drivers get (you) to work!

At the same time, it's important for you to motivate your employees and bring the three drivers of motivation to bear on each individual to the maximum possible extent. Richard Branson once said:

> "I have always believed that the way you treat your employees is the way they will treat your customers, and that people flourish when they are praised."

As a Convincing Communicator, Effective Manager, Motivating Team Leader, Empathetic Psychologist, and Skilled Problem Solver, your ultimate goal is to do everything you can with commitment and dedication, and ensure that employees are doing the same, too. Worldwide, unfortunately, the salary paradigm still prevails in many companies: Instead of praise and good relationships, managers rely on salary increases, monetary benefits, and bonuses as motivational drivers (as if money were the decisive feel-good factor).

Yet countless studies show that there is no significant correlation between salary and job satisfaction. Rather, it's important that employees feel valued and go to work every day with the feeling that they are working on something bigger. People who perform meaningful work have better health, higher life satisfaction, more commitment, and stronger team spirit. They are also less depressed by mistakes and have higher motivation. The leader's greatest task is to bring himself and then the employees into this energetic state. Thus, self-motivation is the key to your success and also the success of your employees.

The many tips in this book and the five roles a leader must master are, at first glance, quite a lot to take in all at once. It will take you a while to perfectly master the roles and tools presented in this book. My best tip: Pick one of the five roles and within that one role, write out the tools you like best. Use these tools quite actively in your everyday work life as a leader, and get into the habit of using them. A month later, choose the next role and do the same thing again. After five months, you'll have tried the tools most important to you in each role and know what works best for you.

Finally, here's my favorite Stephen Covey definition of leadership:

> "Leadership is communicating other's worth and potential so clearly that they are inspired to see it in themselves."

Since I began this section with Goethe, I'll finish it with another quote from him: *"By working within limits does the master truly show himself."* So, limit yourself to the tools you consider most important first, and go on to master the five roles of a leader!

10 Reading Recommendations

1. Cialdini, Robert. *Influence: The Psychology of persuasion.*

2. Covey, Stephen. *7 Habits of Highly Effective People: Powerful Lessons in Personal Change.*

3. Drucker, Peter. *The Effective Executive: The Definitive Guide to Getting the Right Things Done.*

4. Duhigg, Charles. *Smarter Faster Better: The Secrets of Being Productive in Life and Business.*

5. Frankl, Viktor. *Man's Search for Meaning.*

6. Godin, Seth. *Tribes: We Need You to Lead Us.*

7. Goleman, Daniel, Richard Boyatzis and Annie McKee. *Primal Leadership: Unleashing the Power of Emotional Intelligence.*

8. Aurelius, Marcus. *Meditations.*

9. Pink, Daniel. *Drive: The Surprising Truth About What Motivates Us.*

10. Sinek, Simon. *Start with Why: How Great Leaders Inspire Everyone to Take Action.*

About the Author

Wladislaw Jachtchenko is a TOP speaker in Europe. He has been lecturing, training, and coaching politicians and executives from well-known companies for more than a decade, including employees from Allianz, BMW, Pro7, Westwing, and 3M, among many others. His clients learn not only about the tools of professional rhetoric, but also effective persuasion techniques, methods for successful negotiation and professional conflict management, and techniques for effective leadership.

You can book Mr. Jachtchenko for keynote speeches (https://www.wladislaw-jachtchenko.com/en/homepage/), business workshops (https://argumentorik.com/en/workshops/#business) and communication trainings (https://argumentorik.com/en/workshops/#rhetorik). As a 5-star coach, he offers the right mix of theory and practice, significantly improving his clients' communication skills.

Mr. Jachtchenko studied political science, law, modern history, and comparative literature in Munich and New York. A former scholarship holder of the German National Academic Foundation, he's a **fully qualified lawyer** (both state examinations in Bavaria) and **political scientist** (Master of Arts at Columbia University in New York City).

After working as a lawyer in a Munich law firm and as a research assistant at the United Nations in New York, he followed his passion for motivating people and began working as a full-time trainer, speaker, and coach in 2007. His specialties include customized corporate seminars, entertaining rhetoric courses, and intensive coaching on all topics related to leadership & communication.

Mr. Jachtchenko is the **Founder of the Argumentation Academy** (www.argumentorik.com/en/) and developer of the Argumentorik Concept, which puts the coherent argument in the center of every communication and regards rhetoric as an aesthetic tool for a persuasive argumentation.

He is also the author of the top-selling book "Dark Rhetoric: Manipulate Before You're Manipulated!" as well as the innovative communication book "White Rhetoric: Convince Instead of Manipulating", (both in German, published by Goldmann Verlag).

If you would like to get in touch with Mr. Jachtchenko, send him an email at wj@argumentorik.com.

LET'S STAY IN TOUCH!

LinkedIn: https://goo.gl/ZqX4oZ

Facebook: https://www.facebook.com/Argumentorik

Instagram: wlad.argumentorik

YouTube: https://goo.gl/6dQ1ge

Website: https://www.argumentorik.com

Made in the USA
Monee, IL
29 April 2022

95644679R00098